To all the physical educators who are dedicated to teaching children,
all children, may this book help you with your life's work.
To my colleagues who have supported me in this endeavor
and helped me grow through this process.
To my editor, Ms. Judy Wright, who answered hundreds of questions
and kept me on track throughout this endeavor.
To my mentors, who trained me for this profession: Dr. Lane Goodwin,
Dr. Jean Pyfer, Dr. Claudine Sherrill, and Dr. Ronald French.
To my family: my wife, Janelle; sons, Matthew and Timothy;
and daughter, Molly Marie,
whose love and support have made it possible to complete this project.
Finally, I thank God for His many blessings and unconditional love,
and may we always remember those who lost their lives
on September 11, 2001. God bless America.

Contents

Inclusion Index   vii

Preface   ix

Acknowledgments   xiii

How to Use This Book   xv

Part I Fundamentals

1 Legal Background   3

Direct Service   4

Child Find   4

LRE versus Inclusion   5

LRE and Individualized Education Plans (IEPs)   5

2 Wheelchair Basics   7

Wheelchair Mobility Skills   7

Part II Invasion Games

3 Wheelchair Basketball   17

Description of the Sport   17

Skills to Be Taught   21

Functional Profiles and General Modifications   30

Game Progressions   32

Games-by-Skill-Level Index: Low-Functioning Students   32

Game Descriptions   32

Games-by-Skill-Level Index: Moderate- to High-Functioning Students   43

Game Descriptions   44

4 Indoor Wheelchair Soccer   57

Description of the Sport   57

Skills to Be Taught   62

Functional Profiles and General Modifications   69

Game Progressions   70

Games-by-Skill-Level Index: Low-Functioning Students   70

Game Descriptions   71

Games-by-Skill-Level Index: Moderate- to High-Functioning Students   81

Game Descriptions   81

Inclusion Through Sports

Ronald W. Davis, PhD
Ball State University

Human Kinetics

Library of Congress Cataloging-in-Publication Data

Davis, Ronald W., 1950-
 Inclusion through sports / Ronald W. Davis.
  p. cm.
 Includes index.
 ISBN 0-7360-3439-0
 1. Physical education for handicapped persons. 2. Mainstreaming in education. I. Title.

 GV445 .D344 2002
 796.04'56--dc21

            2001051466

ISBN: 0-7360-3439-0

Acquisitions Editor: Judy Patterson Wright, PhD
Developmental Editor: Jennifer Clark
Assistant Editor: Amanda Gunn
Copyeditor: Patsy Fortney
Proofreader: Erin Cler
Indexer: Dan Connolly
Graphic Designer: Nancy Rasmus
Graphic Artist: Kathleen Boudreau-Fuoss
Cover Designer: Dijon Duncan
Photographer (cover): Ronald W. Davis
Art Manager: Carl Johnson
Illustrator: Roberto Sabas
Printer: Versa Press

Printed in the United States of America 10 9 8 7 6 5 4 3 2

Human Kinetics
Web site: www.HumanKinetics.com

United States: Human Kinetics, P.O. Box 5076, Champaign, IL 61825-5076
800-747-4457
e-mail: humank@hkusa.com

Canada: Human Kinetics, 475 Devonshire Road, Unit 100, Windsor, ON N8Y 2L5
800-465-7301 (in Canada only)
e-mail: orders@hkcanada.com

Europe: Human Kinetics, 107 Bradford Road, Stanningley
Leeds LS28 6AT, United Kingdom
+44 (0) 113 255 5665
e-mail: hk@hkeurope.com

Australia: Human Kinetics, 57A Price Avenue, Lower Mitcham, South Australia 5062
08 8277 1555
e-mail: liaw@hkaustralia.com

New Zealand: Human Kinetics, Division of Sports Distributors NZ Ltd.
P.O. Box 300 226 Albany, North Shore City, Auckland
0064 9 448 1207

Part III   Net Games

5 **Sitting Volleyball** **93**

Description of the Sport 94

Skills to Be Taught 97

Functional Profiles and General Modifications 104

Game Progressions 105

Games-by-Skill-Level Index: Low-Functioning Students 105

Game Descriptions 106

Games-by-Skill-Level Index: Moderate- to High-Functioning Students 114

Game Descriptions 115

6 **Wheelchair Tennis** **125**

Description of the Sport 126

Skills to Be Taught 129

Functional Profiles and General Modifications 134

Game Progressions 136

Games-by-Skill-Level Index: Low-Functioning Students 136

Game Descriptions 136

Games-by-Skill-Level Index: Moderate- to High-Functioning Students 143

Game Descriptions 143

Part IV   Court Games/Track Events

7 **Goalball** **151**

Description of the Sport 151

Skills to Be Taught 157

Functional Profiles and General Modifications 160

Game Progressions 161

Games-by-Skill-Level Index: Low-Functioning Students 162

Game Descriptions 162

Games-by-Skill-Level Index: Moderate- to High-Functioning Students 168

Game Descriptions 168

8 **The Slalom** **177**

Description of the Sport 177

Skills to Be Taught 181

Functional Profiles and General Modifications 186

Game Progressions 186

Games-by-Skill-Level Index 187

Game Descriptions 187

Appendix A   Legal Applications   **197**

Appendix B   Wheelchair Basics   **205**

Appendix C   Links to Other Sports and Adapted Activities   **213**

Appendix D   Equipment Concerns   **215**

Suggested Readings   217
Index   219
About the Author   221

Inclusion Index

	Wheelchair Basketball		Sitting Volleyball		Goalball
	Indoor Wheelchair Soccer		Wheelchair Tennis		The Slalom (Track)

Parts of the Book	Sports in General Physical Education Curriculum	Using Disability Sports			
Part II: Invasion Games	**Basketball**				
	Passing				
	Dribbling				
	Shooting				
	Ball movement				
	Soccer				
	Passing				
	Dribbling				
	Throw-in				
	Blocking				

(continued)

(continued)

Parts of the Book	Sports in General Physical Education Curriculum	Using Disability Sports			
Part III: Net Games	**Volleyball**				
	Serve	Sitting Volleyball	Wheelchair Tennis		
	Bump/pass	Sitting Volleyball	Goalball		
	Set	Sitting Volleyball			
	Block	Sitting Volleyball	Goalball	Indoor Wheelchair Soccer	
	Tennis				
	Forehand	Wheelchair Tennis			
	Backhand	Wheelchair Tennis			
	Serve	Wheelchair Tennis	Sitting Volleyball		
Part IV: Court Games/Track Events	**Track and Field**				
	Sprints	The Slalom (Track)	Goalball		
	Relays	The Slalom (Track)			
	Throw	Goalball			

Preface

If you are a general physical education teacher with minimal or no training in adapted physical education and are being asked to teach students with disabilities, this book is for you. It will help you develop programs for students with disabilities using games and activities derived from the field of disability sport. With the information presented here, you will be able to establish a comprehensive physical education program for students with and without disabilities using the medium of sport.

Sport Is Universal

Sport is a universal language that is understood, respected, and practiced around the world. Inclusive sport can be a way to bridge the gap between students with and without disabilities in your physical education classes. By implementing the suggestions from this book, you will not only provide appropriate services to students with disabilities, but you will also broaden your curriculum for all students.

The field of disability sport appears to be untapped by general physical educators. Most physical educators can identify Special Olympics as a program that provides sporting opportunities for individuals with mental retardation. They are familiar with its organizational structure, competitions, and individual sport skills, but how many can name other disability sport organizations? How many of us can name the sport organizations that represent individuals with spinal cord injuries, amputations, cerebral palsy, or visual impairments? This book will introduce you to disability sports (and their organizations) and help you apply them to your curriculum. It will show you how to teach the skills needed to play each sport successfully, and have fun doing it.

What would you do if you had a student who was blind or had a visual impairment in your physical education class during a volleyball unit? You might try to modify the game using a ball with an auditory device, but that is difficult to create out of a typical volleyball. Why not supplement the unit of volleyball with skills from the game of goalball for that student? Goalball? What is goalball, and how can the skills of goalball be used in my current curriculum? Good question. Chapter 7 explains the skills needed to play goalball and provides specific activities to help supplement your curriculum with this sport. How would you include a student who uses a wheelchair in a volleyball unit? Have you heard of sitting volleyball? Read chapter 5 and learn more about sitting volleyball to find out its application to your curriculum. Chapter 3 is about wheelchair basketball and demonstrates how basketball skills can be taught to students with and without disabilities.

Sport Skills

The disability sports selected for this book are for students with physical or sensory impairments and were chosen, in part, due to their popularity. Because all of them have competitions at the national and/or international level, your students with *and* without disabilities will have the opportunity to observe role models in the sports. By using these sports in your curriculum, you will be presenting skills that students with and without disabilities have a greater opportunity to engage in throughout their lifetime.

The sport skills associated with these disability sports are broken down to their simplest forms to help you address the needs of students with disabilities. For example, let's take the task of teaching a student how to shoot a basketball. All students require some functional level of "grasp and release" to shoot a basketball. For a student with a disability, the functional level of grasp and release might preclude that student from successfully shooting a basketball. In chapter 3, two of the games suggested in the skill level index for low-functioning students are Hanging On and Shot's Away. These activities will help you address the functional need of grasp and release for a student with a disability in your basketball unit.

Statement on Inclusion

Making students with disabilities part of the decision-making process is the core of this book's philosophical approach to inclusion. Physical education is meant to address three domains of learning: psychomotor, cognitive, and affective. The inclusion suggestions found in the following chapters are designed to address all three domains. I believe we can include students with disabilities by implementing modifications to address motor limitations (psychomotor). We can, for example, shorten base paths or lower nets for students with movement limitations and minimal upper-body strength. But we should not assume that such physical modifications address the remaining two domains (cognitive and affective). Unless we provide specific tasks directed at emphasizing all three domains, our inclusion attempts will be incomplete. To include a student with a disability in your physical education program, you must address all three domains. Your activities should create opportunities for students with disabilities to share in the decision-making process with their nondisabled peers.

About the Book

The book is organized into four parts (Fundamentals, Invasion Games, Net Games, and Court Games/Track Events) and eight chapters, six of which deal specifically with disability sport.

Part I: Fundamentals

Chapter 1 presents a brief explanation of the legislative responsibilities for the general physical educator serving students with disabilities. It begins with a brief review of the legislative mandates that have affected physical education for students with disabilities, then addresses your involvement with the individualized education plan (IEP). Appendix A offers suggestions on how to apply the information from this book to the IEP process and how you can get more actively involved.

Chapter 2 is about wheelchair mobility skills generic to wheelchair sports. Teaching students with disabilities basic wheelchair mobility skills might be very appropriate for some students and can provide valuable lessons for teachers to use at any point in the curriculum. Wheelchair mobility skills such as self-propulsion, stopping, and performing a stationary or moving pivot are essential for students who use manual wheelchairs. Appendix B provides information about wheelchair selection and operation and fitting a student properly for a wheelchair.

Part II: Invasion Games

Invasion games are games that feature teamwork and some type of offensive strategy to invade a defended goal area. The defense must react to an offensive "attack" near the defended goal area. In chapters 3 and 4, wheelchair basketball and indoor wheelchair soccer are presented as invasion games.

Part III: Net Games

Net games are those designed to be played on a court using a net to separate two teams or individuals. The net becomes part of the offensive and defensive strategy. Chapters 5 and 6 describe sitting volleyball and wheelchair tennis, respectively. Skills similar to those required in regulation volleyball and tennis will be presented, with specific disability sport emphasis on court size and rules of the games.

Part IV: Court Games/Track Events

The last part of the book includes games played indoors and outside on flat, level surfaces. Chapters 7 and 8 include the sport of goalball and the slalom. Goalball is a sport played by individuals who are blind or visually impaired, and the slalom is designed for individuals with severe disabilities who use power or electric wheelchairs. The slalom offers a unique alternative for your track unit.

Acknowledgments

I would like to thank the following professionals for their contributions to this book. They have contributed their reviews, critiques, and professional opinions on their respective sports, and I sincerely appreciate their efforts.

Sport	Professional
Wheelchair Basketball	Mr. Ronald Lykins NWBA and USA Paralympic Coach
	Mr. Frank Burns NWBA Executive Director
Indoor Wheelchair Soccer	Mr. Bill Wilkie NDSA Coach
	Mr. Jerry McCole NDSA Executive Director
Sitting Volleyball	Mr. Michael Hulett USA Sitting Volleyball Coach
Wheelchair Tennis	Mr. Miles Thompson Lakeshore Foundation Tennis Instructor
	Mr. Randy Snow Wheelchair Tennis Player, Coach, Author
Goalball	Dr. Thomas Weidner National Goalball Team
The Slalom	Mr. Bill Wilkie NDSA Coach

Others

I wish to thank the following individuals for demonstrating the skills presented in this book.

Sport/Activity	Individual
Wheelchair Basketball	Ms. Patty Cisneros USA 2000 Paralympic Wheelchair Basketball Team
	Ms. Karen Wake USA 2000 Paralympic Wheelchair Basketball Team
Indoor Wheelchair Soccer	Mr. Michael Gillam Ball State University Student
	Ms. Amanda Campbell Ball State University Graduate Student

Sport/Activity	Individual
Sitting Volleyball	Ms. Molly Davis Ms. Lauren Kaminsky Ms. Nadia Tabari Burris Middle School
Wheelchair Tennis	Mr. Tim Davis Burris Middle School
Goalball	Dr. Thomas Weidner National Goalball Team
The Slalom	Mr. Hector Garcia Ball State University Student
Wheelchair Fitting	Mr. Matthew Davis Burris High School/Indiana Academy Ms. Molly Davis Burris Middle School
Wheelchair Mobility	Mr. Tim Davis Burris Middle School

How to Use This Book

The basic philosophy of this book is choice—your choice. This book is not written to be a "how to teach" text, but rather is designed to be a supplementary text to your current curriculum. The following five steps are meant to help you either adopt an entire disability sport into your curriculum or integrate selected sport skills from designated disability sports. If you choose to adopt a disability sport, you may elect to supplement your entire curriculum by adding a unit on wheelchair basketball or sitting volleyball for all students to learn. Or you may elect to integrate a disability sport into your curriculum by teaching only one or two skills from wheelchair basketball, such as the bounce stop or bounce spin, to students who use wheelchairs. Remember, the choice is yours; be open minded and ready to let your creativity arise. Feel free to think outside of the box.

Step 1: Locate a Sport

Locate a sport that is represented in your current curriculum by using the inclusion index on page vii. The inclusion index is organized according to parts II, III, and IV of this book (Invasion Games, Net Games, and Court Games/Track Events). The inclusion index should help you decide which disability sport(s) or sport skill(s) to use in your general physical education curriculum. Each disability sport is represented by an icon printed at the top of the index. Basketball, soccer, volleyball, tennis, and track/field serve as the basic sports that are assumed to be taught in an upper elementary or secondary school's general physical education curriculum. The icons for the disability sports are cross-referenced to the sports of the general physical education curriculum.

Step 2: Cross-Reference a Disability Sport

To use the inclusion index, simply find the sport or sport skill you are interested in teaching or are currently teaching in your general curriculum, and cross-reference this skill to the disability sport or sport skill using the icons from each sport. Once you have determined the appropriate disability sport(s) or sport skill(s), refer to the appropriate chapter and follow the information presented.

For example, let's say you are currently teaching a basketball unit and working on the skill of passing. You have a student who uses a wheelchair, and you need additional ideas to help with this skill. Turn to chapter 3 and read about three different passes taught in wheelchair basketball, then read how each can be used in a game or activity.

If you have a student who has a visual impairment in that same basketball class, you might elect to read about the skill of passing for goalball in chapter 7. Turn to chapter 7, read about goalball, then read about the specific skill of passing used during the game. Suggested games to emphasize passing in goalball follow the skill descriptions.

Step 3: Learn About the Game and Its Skills

Once you have cross-referenced the disability sport or sport skill you are interested in, you need to learn about the game. Each chapter begins with a narrative about the sport called Description of the Sport followed by a brief summary of the sport in chart form. The description of the sport includes the following information: field of play, players, equipment, starting the game, game objective, game length, general rules, rules specific to the sport, and a summary. In the next section, Skills to Be Taught, you will read about and view selected skills deemed important for this sport. Each skill is task-analyzed and supported with an illustration to help with instruction.

Step 4: Match Your Student's Functional Level of Performance

Once you are familiar with the sport and the skills to be taught, you need to assess your student's functional level of performance. To help you with this task, each chapter has a student functional profile table organized according to functional ability. The functional profiles are organized into low, moderate, and high categories. These profiles have been operationally defined and modified according to each sport's official classification system. They are meant to be general guidelines for you in your game selection. Once you have matched your student's functional profile, each chapter offers general modifications to be taught. Specific activities follow in step 5.

Step 5: Select and Implement an Appropriate Game

Specific games are referenced in each chapter according to the student's functional level and sequence of game progressions. The chapters have two games-by-skill-level indexes that offer specific games according to the game level you feel is appropriate for your student based on their functional level. The first index is for students with low functional ability, and the second is for those with moderate to high functional ability. Once you have chosen the appropriate index, you simply find the skill to be addressed and cross-reference it with the game level according to the game progressions.

Game progressions have three levels: individual, small group, and teamwork. The individual level is meant for the student to accomplish before working in small groups. Small group activities can engage two to three students and should include students with and without disabilities. Teamwork activities can engage three to five or more students working together for a single objective. Each game description includes the following sections: game level, formation, equipment, description, extensions, and inclusion suggestions.

Summary

Some of the disability sport skills described in this book may not appear to the traditionalist to be appropriate for the suggested nondisabled sports unit. For example, allowing a student with a visual impairment to work on goalball skills during a basketball unit may seem out of the ordinary, but I assure you it is highly effective. Since goalball is a game a person with a visual impairment would be more likely to play later in life, it is logical to teach the skill of passing a ball using that game rather than through basketball, a sport that individual is not likely to play later.

Not all students with disabilities are going to fit into this book's suggestions. Some students will need rather detailed modifications, and some will not. The suggestions in this book are meant to offer you a direction, a focus, a mechanism to begin appropriate programming for students with disabilities in your general physical education class. You have the choice of how to implement the disability sport into your curriculum. Remember, creativity and imagination will be the keys to your success.

PART I

FUNDAMENTALS

Chapter 1   Legal Background

Chapter 2   Wheelchair Basics

1

Legal Background

In the 1970s Americans began to see changes for minority populations in the workplace and in schools. Gender equity was established in sport under Title IX, and the educational rights of individuals with disabilities were emerging through a new discipline called special education. The genesis of special education can be traced to the passage of Public Law 94-142 (PL 94-142) in 1975, titled the Education Act for Handicapped Children. Little did we realize the far-reaching effects this piece of legislation would have on us as physical educators.

PL 94-142 mandated appropriate education, including physical education, for all children with disabilities in all educational disciplines. Physical educators were faced with integrating special education, with its terminology and concepts, into their discipline. This task has proved to be a challenge since its inception. General physical educators have had to become familiar with terms and concepts such as individualized education plan (IEP), least restrictive environment (LRE), mainstreaming, and inclusion. Mandates to learn new vocabulary and instructional practices made the transition of working with students with disabilities challenging for the untrained general physical educator. Despite this challenge, some physical educators forged ahead and sought to learn about special education.

The material presented in this chapter is based on the assumption that you are interested in reviewing how special education relates to your teaching situation. The objective of this chapter is to review basic information surrounding the educational process for students with disabilities. This chapter will not teach you how to write an IEP or conduct a formal motor assessment. Practical ways for you to better engage the special education process are presented in appendix A, which is designed to help you apply the suggestions to your teaching situation.

While PL 94-142 brought about several basic educational rights for children with disabilities, including physical education, professional consensus is that several other issues were central to its purpose. The law helped establish the categories of disabilities to be considered eligible for special education services. Originally, these categories included people who were mentally retarded, hard of hearing, deaf, speech impaired, visually impaired, emotionally disturbed, orthopedically impaired, other health impaired, learning disabled, deaf-blind, and multihandicapped. Later, two additional categories were added for people with autism and traumatic brain injury. The law further established the ages of eligible service. Originally, the ages of service were 3 to 21 years. Several years later the age range was increased to include birth to 21 years. However, the issue that physical educators needed to be aware of then, and perhaps still do today, is the concept of direct service.

Direct Service

As of this writing, the law states that special education is ". . . specially designed instruction at no cost to the parent, to meet the unique needs of the student with disabilities, including instruction in the classroom, home instruction, instruction in hospitals and institutions, and *instruction in physical education.*" (Emphasis added.) The fact that physical education is the only curriculum area specifically mentioned in the definition of special education is the basis for its interpretation of being a direct service. Direct services are classes or course offerings that must be made available to students with disabilities, at no cost to their parents, if those same classes are offered to students without disabilities. So if students without disabilities have the opportunity for physical education classes, then students with disabilities must receive the same opportunity.

Notice that the curriculum identified is *physical education* and not *physical therapy* or *occupational therapy*. Physical and occupational therapy are identified in the law as related services, or services established to aid in the delivery of direct services. So it was the intent of the law for students with disabilities to receive physical education (a direct service) before any related services would be implemented. However, school district administrators and building principals have not always held to that mandate. Many times physical therapy has been offered in place of physical education to students with disabilities, which is a clear violation of the law.

Child Find

In order to establish the most appropriate service for students with disabilities, PL 94-142 created a process referred to as Child Find. The Child Find process is an all-encompassing process that includes two key components: assessment and least restrictive environment placement.

Assessment

For the physical educator, assessment means making evaluations in several areas of physical education. Students with disabilities have to be assessed in areas such as fundamental motor skills; physical and motor fitness; and skills needed for participation in individual and team games, aquatics, sports, and dance. Such a task is difficult for the physical educator whose professional training in this area has been minimal. Professionals trained in adapted physical education are better qualified to assess the individual needs of students with disabilities.

Least Restrictive Environment (LRE)

Once the assessment aspect is completed, the information has to be evaluated and a decision made as to where the child with a disability should be placed for education service. Physical educators must now decide what the best learning environment or least restrictive environment (LRE) for the child would be.

Given the wide range of children with disabilities, the LRE interpretations are up for debate. However, many professionals agree on the following examples of LRE placements for physical education: (1) the general physical education classroom, (2) part-time in the general physical education classroom and part-time in an adapted environment, (3) part-time in general physical education and full-time in an adapted environment, (4) full-time in adapted physical education, or (5) full-time in specialty schools such as schools for the blind or deaf. Professionals have also struggled with defining LRE in the context of inclusion.

LRE Versus Inclusion

Inclusion was first and foremost an educational reform, a philosophy; it was never mandated by law. Only the concept of least restrictive environment was mandated by PL 94-142. Inclusion is the practice of educating students with and without disabilities in general education classes. Students with disabilities are placed in the general physical education class as their initial educational placement. With inclusion, there is no continuum of placement options or initial assessment practice to determine LRE. Such assessment practices occur after the child has been placed in the general setting. Inclusion requires providing the general classroom teacher with a continuum of support services in order to make the educational placement successful for the student with a disability. For physical education that support comes in the form of special equipment, trained therapists (physical or occupational therapists), adapted physical educators, or paraprofessionals (trained teacher assistants).

LRE and Individualized Education Plans (IEPs)

To continue with the LRE process, once the evaluation or assessment is complete, the teachers and parents need a guide or management plan. The management plan is the individualized education plan, or IEP. The IEP contains several key components that document how to progress the student with a disability through their educational experience. Among the most prevalent of the components are these three: (1) present-level statement, (2) statement of annual goal, and (3) short-term objectives. Physical educators must write, based on their assessments, at least these three components and then share them with other professionals during a meeting called the case conference or IEP meeting. Professionals from various disciplines converge at this meeting to report their assessment information of the child. For example, professionals from reading, math, science, and physical education may meet with parents and school administrators to present their assessment results and make their recommendations for the child's educational placement.

It is critical for you as a physical educator reading this book to get involved with the IEP process. Because your contributions are important for an overall picture of the child, you should be prepared to report and share information at an IEP meeting. Examples of how to use the material in this book for an IEP are presented in appendix A. Your students with disabilities are counting on you; don't miss the opportunity to contribute to their education.

2

Wheelchair Basics

When integrating students with disabilities into your physical education class, you should first address the issue of how the wheelchair is perceived by students without disabilities. By viewing the wheelchair as an extension of the person using it, as simply a different way to move, you encourage your students without disabilities to do the same. It is important to get your students without disabilities to see the person using the wheelchair, and not the wheelchair itself. The wheelchair helps define the individual using it; it is a differentiating characteristic to be considered along with eye and hair color, height, and weight. When you as the general physical educator create an environment in your classes that supports such an attitude, the attitude spills over onto the other students in your classes.

Wheelchair Mobility Skills

Five basic maneuvers should be considered essential movements for students who use manual wheelchairs. These skills could be taught as part of a physical education class for students with disabilities within the general curriculum. These same skills could also be taught to students without disabilities who might be involved in learning a disability sport. The five movement skills are forward propulsion, stopping, backward propulsion, the stationary pivot or spin, and the moving pivot or spin. Each skill will be highlighted by key teaching points. The mainwheel of the wheelchair is referenced as the face of a clock. Therefore, if the teaching suggestion mentions positioning the student's hands at 12 o'clock, that should be interpreted as placing the hands at the top of the mainwheel.

Forward Propulsion

To begin with, all references to pushing a wheelchair should be made from the perspective of the individual doing the pushing and not from the perspective of being pushed. Pushing a wheelchair is described in two phases: propulsion and recovery. The propulsive phase is when the individual exerts force onto the handrims, driving the wheelchair forward. Using the clockface reference, the propulsion phase is approximately from 12 o'clock to 5 o'clock. The recovery phase begins at the end of propulsion, or between 5 and 6 o'clock. The recovery phase begins as the hands break contact with the handrims and move back up to the beginning of the propulsive phase, or approximately 11 or 12 o'clock.

When teaching the propulsive phase, it is important for you to emphasize starting the hands at top dead center of the mainwheel. As the student makes contact with the handrims and tires, they should push with the pads of their hands and rest their thumbs on the tires, keeping the fingers slightly curled under the handrim. As the student begins to push, make sure the elbows, shoulders, and hands are in alignment, ready for the elbows to be extended forward with force. As the elbows are extended, the student flexes the trunk slightly with shoulders over the tires and drives the hands and elbows forward and down, using trunk flexion to reach forward. As the hands reach forward and downward as far as possible, the student pushes through at least one quarter of the wheel's circumference and gets ready for the recovery phase. To execute the recovery phase, the student releases the hands from the rims briefly in order to return to the start position and focuses on returning the hands to the rims as quickly as possible. Remember, hands off the rims means no force is applied, and no force to the handrims means the wheelchair is slowing down, so emphasize maximizing propulsion phases and minimizing recovery phases.

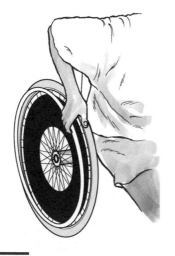

Hand position on tire and rim for forward propulsion.

Body position to begin forward propulsion.

Begin recovery phase.

Recovery phase.

Reposition hands for next forward propulsion.

Stopping the Wheelchair

The second wheelchair mobility skill to learn is to properly stop the wheelchair and keep control. All disability sports that use a wheelchair require a high degree of wheelchair control. Players unable to maintain control of their wheelchairs could be penalized or ruled out of control.

To teach proper stopping techniques, start the student from the basic position described in forward propulsion. As the wheelchair is moving forward, the student leans forward as far as possible and grips both wheels simultaneously. As the student secures a solid grip, they pull back on the wheels simultaneously by wrapping their fingers around the handrims. To control the stop, the student leans backward as the pull is made, maintaining an equal pull and balanced sitting positioned. Those individuals with weak abdominal support should consider using special strapping for support during competition, as sudden stopping could cause the individual to fall from the wheelchair.

Grip both wheels for stopping.

Lean back to control the stop.

Backward Propulsion

Backward propulsion is used quite often in several wheelchair sport team games, such as wheelchair basketball and indoor wheelchair soccer. Backward propulsion allows the player to keep their body in a good position to see the court and the action taking place around them. This skill helps the player to maintain better control of their wheelchair and allows them to see dangers that could be avoided. The basic technique of this maneuver is a pulling type of motion.

To begin the backward propulsion maneuver, the student should be in the basic sitting position described for stopping the wheelchair. To initiate the backward propulsion, the student leans forward and reaches down on the handrims as low as possible, gripping the main tires. The student's shoulders should be directly over the hands and all joints involved with the movement should be in alignment (that is, wrist, elbows, and shoulders). Next, the student uses short, quick pulls backward on the wheels making sure to keep the pulling movement symmetrical. Because the front steering wheels (casters) are trailing, keeping the wheelchair under control is difficult, so the student shouldn't move too rapidly. As backward movement takes place, the student keeps their body weight forward and balanced over the knees. Make sure to instruct the student not to lean back too far as they initiate the pulling motion, as such movement could cause the wheelchair to tip over.

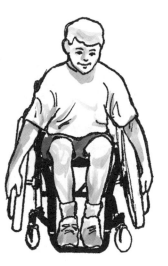 

Reach forward to begin the reverse pull.   Pull back symmetrically.

Stationary Pivot (Spin)

This maneuver is essential for helping a student change directions quickly during a game or activity. The stationary pivot or spin is performed by using a push-pull technique in coordination with proper weight shift. The direction of spin is determined by which wheel is pulled and which wheel is pushed. The spin will always move in the direction of the pulled wheel. The stationary pivot is taught from the basic forward propulsion position described earlier. The stationary pivot is the basic movement for the bounce stop and bounce spin used in wheelchair basketball (chapter 3).

To execute the stationary pivot, the student extends one arm down the handrim of the tire on the side of the intended spin (right arm for a pivot to the right). The opposite

Extend pivot arm down, ready to pull.

Position pushing arm at 12 o'clock.

Push-pull to spin the wheelchair.

Continue to push-pull through the spin.

arm is placed at 12 o'clock on the opposite tire, or top dead center, and in a ready position to push. To initiate the movement, the student pulls up with the extended arm (right) and pushes with the opposite arm (left) simultaneously; this should spin the wheelchair. To complete the spin move, the student's pulling arm (right) should pass the top dead center of the right wheel, keeping in contact with the handrim. This same arm is now ready to initiate a new forward propulsion movement.

Moving Pivot (Spin)

This skill is performed in the same way as the stationary pivot, except that the student must now shift their body over to the side of the intended pivot during the pulling action. This is accomplished by leaning to one side and maintaining trunk stability so as not to fall from the wheelchair. To execute a right-hand moving pivot, the student shifts the

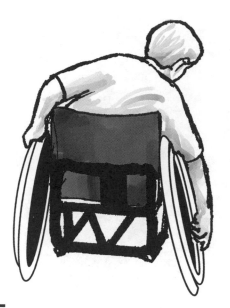

Shift body weight to the side of the pivot.

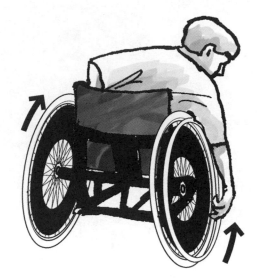

Push-pull to spin the wheelchair.

body weight to the right side of the wheelchair while moving and pulls back on the right wheel, making sure the pulling hand passes top dead center, or 12 o'clock. As the right-hand pivot is made, the student uses the pivot hand to initiate a new forward propulsion movement. Students with poor trunk stability should consider using support strapping to assist with balance. By shifting the body weight, the student places more weight over the turning side, which helps to control the moving wheelchair and executes this dynamic skill.

Summary

The following set of tables can be used as quick references for points discussed in this chapter. Use them to help set up teaching stations or skill checklists.

Teaching points	Forward Wheelchair Propulsion
	1. Hands are positioned at top dead center.
	2. Pads of hands and thumbs are resting on tires, fingers slightly curled under handrims.
	3. Elbows, shoulders, hands are in alignment, ready for elbows to be extended forward.
	4. Trunk is slightly flexed, with shoulders over the tires.
	5. Drive hands and elbows forward and down, using trunk flexion to reach forward.
	6. Push hands through the drive phase for at least one quarter of the wheel's circumference.

Wheelchair Stopping Technique

1. Start from the basic position described in the forward propulsion position.
2. Reach forward with both arms and grip the wheels as low as possible.
3. Pull back on the wheels simultaneously by wrapping the fingers around the handrims and gripping tightly.
4. Lean trunk backward while pulling up and back with both arms.
5. Individuals with weak abdominal support should consider using special strapping for support during competition. Sudden stopping could cause the individual to fall from the wheelchair.

Backward Wheelchair Propulsion

1. Start from the basic position described in the reach position of the stopping skill.
2. Reach forward with both arms, flexing the trunk and gripping the wheel as in the forward propulsion.
3. Shoulders should be directly over the hands on the rim, and all joints involved (wrist, elbows, shoulders) should be in alignment.
4. Pull back using short, quick pulls.
5. The steering wheels of the wheelchair (casters) are now trailing, thus making maneuvering difficult. Keep the body weight forward and balanced over the knees if possible to avoid leaning too far back and tipping the wheelchair over.

Stationary Wheelchair Pivot (Spin)

1. Extend the arm downward to the side intended to spin.
2. Position the opposite hand at 12 o'clock on the opposite wheel.
3. Pull the extended arm backward while pushing the opposite arm forward and down.
4. Follow through with the spin by making sure the pulling arm passes top dead center of wheel and remains in contact with the rim as it passes the trunk.
5. As the pulling hand and arm pass backward, keep the hand in contact with the rim. Use the same arm to initiate a push phase in the new position.

Moving Wheelchair Pivot (Spin)

1. Start from the same position as the stationary pivot.
2. As the spin is executed, shift the weight to the intended direction of movement.
3. Pull back on the wheel and keep the hand in contact with the rim as it passes top dead center, or 12 o'clock.
4. As the pivot is made, use the pull hand to initiate a new push phase.
5. Students with poor trunk stability should consider using strapping to assist with balance.

PART II

INVASION GAMES

Chapter 3   Wheelchair Basketball

Chapter 4   Indoor Wheelchair Soccer

chapter

3

Wheelchair Basketball

Wheelchair basketball is considered the most widely organized and recognized of all the wheelchair sports. The National Wheelchair Basketball Association (NWBA) was founded in 1948 and has continued to grow across all levels of competition. The NWBA is organized into three divisions for men (I, II, III) and additional divisions for women, collegiate, and youth. Currently 181 teams compete in 22 different conferences across the United States. The collegiate division includes such participants as the University of Illinois, Wright State University, the University of Texas at Arlington, Southwest State University in Minnesota, and the University of Wisconsin at Whitewater. More than 25 teams compete in the youth division from several states including Arkansas, California, Minnesota, Missouri, New Jersey, Texas, Washington, and Wisconsin. Wheelchair basketball is also played at the international level as evidenced in the Paralympics and World Championships. The Paralympics are the Olympic-level competition for individuals with physical and sensory impairments.

Description of the Sport

Wheelchair basketball has many similarities to basketball. It is played on a regulation court using regulation backboards and rims. Players shoot from regulation free-throw and three-point lines. There are five players per team on the floor at any one time using a regulation size basketball. The wheelchair is considered part of the player's body. Contacts with other players for the purpose of gaining an advantage, such as blocking fouls, charging fouls, or out-of-bounds touches, are considered infractions. The game is started with a jump ball at center circle, and the possession rule follows as in regulation basketball. Time limits for in-bounding the ball and crossing the ball over half court are the same as in regulation basketball. A 35-second shooting clock is used in the men's and women's divisions.

Field of Play

The game is played on a regulation court measuring 94 feet by 50 feet with a 19-foot-9-inch three-point line. Not all basketball courts measure the same, so you have to be able to adjust to your facility.

Players

Any person with a permanent lower-body impairment who cannot play regulation basketball while standing is eligible to compete in wheelchair basketball. Individuals with spinal cord injuries, amputations, polio, or other similar conditions are all eligible to play the game. The NWBA recognizes three levels of player classification based on the location of the individual's impairment. Generally speaking, those individuals with spinal cord injuries in the neck and shoulder region would be in Class I. Player's with injuries in the upper to lower thorax would be in Class II, and those injured from the lower thorax and below would be in Class III. For the most part, individuals in Class III are the highest functioning players, while those in Class I are the lowest functioning. Player classification is a factor when fielding a team for an official wheelchair basketball game sponsored by the NWBA. Player classifications are used to define student functional profiles discussed later in this chapter.

Equipment

A player's wheelchair is considered part of their body. The game is played with a regulation size basketball for men and a reduced size basketball for women and youth.

Starting the Game

The game is started with a jump ball at the center circle. There are five players on the floor for each team.

Game Objective

Once the game has been started, the objective is to shoot the ball into your team's basket. Shots made from the floor are scored as two points, as in regulation basketball. Successful free-throw shots are worth one point, and all bonus situations related to team fouls are the same. A shot made from beyond the three-point line is counted as three points; however, it would be your decision to use such a shot. The three-point shot is used in all divisions of the NWBA.

As play continues, each team moves the ball up and down the court in an attempt to either score a basket or stop the opponent. You may consider assigning player positions such as guard, center, and forward as in regulation basketball, but it is not necessary. For the purposes of this book, the recommendation is to provide the students with and without disabilities the opportunity to experience the game without an overemphasis on the positions of play.

Defensive positions on the court are usually presented in either a player-to-player defense or a zone format, similar to regulation basketball. One key point related to defensive positions is "transition play," which is movement from defense to offense, or offense to defense. You should teach your students to move as quickly as possible from offense to defense once a shot has been taken by an opponent. Several of the passing skills mentioned in this chapter, such as the chest, hook, and bounce, will help with that.

Offensive positions on court are also similar to those in regulation basketball. Players at competitive levels try to perfect their shots from a distance of three to six feet from the basket. Since shooting the basketball from more than 12 feet is very difficult and often unproductive, try to emphasize close-range shooting. Several of the skills presented in this chapter, such as shooting and the bounce stop, should help with this task.

General ball movement is accomplished by dribbling or passing. The pass should be the key method of ball movement. Passing can be effective with the half-court offense or when students must transition from one end of the court to the other. Too much dribbling can be costly, so students should be encouraged to work on passing the ball from player to player. Two additional skills that should help ball movement are the bounce spin and ball retrieval. Both of these skills can be effective either to allude defensive players (bounce spin) or to assist with transition during a turnover by the other team (ball retrieval).

Game Length

The NWBA uses regulation game length for its competition, generally two 20-minute halves for men, women, and collegiate, and four 6-minute quarters for youth. You may use whatever time allotments work for your situation.

General Rules/Penalties

As previously mentioned, most rules are similar to those of regulation basketball; however, a few are specific to wheelchair basketball.

Rules Specific to Wheelchair Basketball

If a player falls out of the wheelchair, play is continued unless the fall endangers the fallen player or other players. Players who can right themselves without assistance must be allowed to do so; no assistance from a coach is allowed on the floor. For players who cannot right themselves and return to play, play is stopped to allow a coach to assist.

Players may not rise up from the seat to gain an advantage such as attempting to reach for a ball during a rebound. Lifting of the buttocks from the seat to gain an advantage during a game results in a technical foul shot for the opponent.

A player with the ball may not push the wheelchair wheels more than twice in succession with one or both hands without bouncing the ball to the floor again. Taking more than two consecutive pushes while in possession of the ball constitutes a traveling violation. Players may dribble and push the wheelchair simultaneously just as in regulation basketball. Players who can may execute one push and glide the length of the court while holding the basketball without dribbling, but on the next touch to their handrims they then have to execute a dribble, pass, or shot. There is no double-dribble rule in wheelchair basketball.

The player or any part of the wheelchair besides the wheels may not come in contact with the floor while the player has possession of the ball. If this occurs, a turnover is awarded. A turnover occurs when a player in possession of the ball somehow tips forward in their wheelchair such that the footplates of the wheelchair make contact with the floor. Also, a player is considered out of bounds if any body part or part of the wheelchair touches the outside of the boundary line.

If a player is positioned in the free-throw lane for longer than four seconds during their team's offensive possession, it is considered a lane violation and the ball is awarded to the other team as a turnover. (A lane violation in regulation basketball is three seconds.)

Summary of the Sport

Table 3.1 provides a quick reference to the sport of wheelchair basketball.

Table 3.1	Overview of Wheelchair Basketball
Field of play	Basketball court: 50 ft by 94 ft and no larger than 50 ft by 100 ft Goal height: 10 ft (8.5 ft for youth) Three-point line: 19 ft 9 in.
Players	Maximum allowed on court is five players.
Equipment	Regulation basketball for men Regulation basketball for women and youth
Legal start	The game is started with a center jump.
Ball movement	A player may use only their hands to move the ball. A player may dribble the ball with one hand. A player may not push or touch the handrims more than two consecutive times without dribbling, passing, or shooting the ball. More than two consecutive pushes or touches to the handrim without dribbling is considered traveling, which results in a turnover. A player may not touch the playing surface while in possession of the ball.
Free throws	All players are on each side of the free-throw lane, with team members alternated. A member of the opposing team must be allowed first position closest to the basket. All lane players can go in upon the release of the shot, but the shooter must wait until the ball touches the rim.
Blocking versus charging	Blocking is a legal move and is defined as any player positioning their wheelchair to impede another player's movement. The player must have established position first. Charging is an illegal move defined as a collision from any angle in which a player fails to gain position first or fails to control their own wheelchair at any time. Players are expected to maintain control of their wheelchairs at all times.
Loss of possession	The following result in the loss of possession to the victimized team: • Traveling: More than two consecutive touches to the handrim without a dribble or pass • Any time any part of the wheelchair, other than the wheels, touches the floor • Offensive player considered charging another player

Skills to Be Taught

This section will help you establish your teaching emphasis as you read the basic skills necessary to play wheelchair basketball. Six skills could be taught in your physical education class to students with and without disabilities. Notice that the skill of passing has three variations: chest, bounce, and hook. For students with higher function, you may also use a fourth pass called the baseball pass. The baseball pass is presented in chapter 4, "Indoor Wheelchair Soccer." Dribbling is also broken down into two distinct types: stationary and continuous. There are also three skills essential to the game of wheelchair basketball that rely on general wheelchair mobility: the bounce stop, the bounce spin, and ball retrieval. It is up to you to decide which skills are within the capabilities of your students with disabilities.

Passing

Following are descriptions of three types of passes used in the game of wheelchair basketball. Teach the skills that are most appropriate to your students' abilities.

- **Chest Pass.** Students place their hands on either side of the ball, then draw the ball into the chest by flexing the elbows. Students then extend the elbows forcefully to pass the ball, turning the thumbs inward and down upon release.

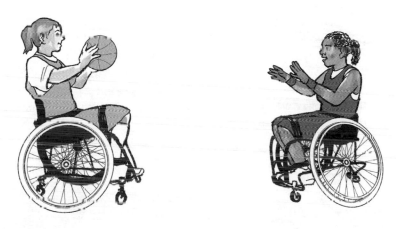

Preparation for two-handed chest pass: eyes on target; elbows flexed.

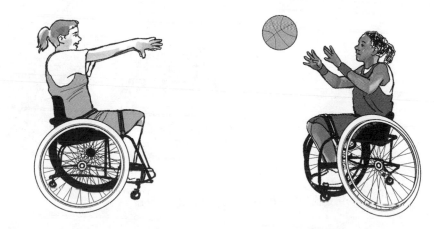

Execution of two-handed chest pass: elbows extended; thumbs point downward.

- **Bounce Pass.** This pass uses the same mechanics as those used in the chest pass, with the following emphasis: students pass the ball so that the bounce hits a spot on the floor halfway between themselves and another student and try to land the ball in the other student's lap.

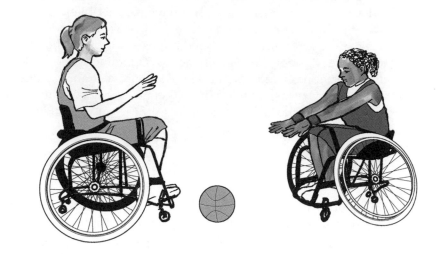

Bounce the ball into a partner's lap.

- **Hook Pass.** This pass is used in a stationary situation when a defensive player is positioned between two offensive players. The offensive player holds the ball in the hand away from the defensive player by extending the arm out and away from the body. The player stabilizes the body by gripping the top of the mainwheel with the hand closest to the defensive player. Using a hooking motion, the player brings the arm with the ball up and over the head so that the elbow of the passing arm strikes the ear upon release of the ball.

Hold the ball up and away from the opponent.

Stabilize the wheelchair with the opposite hand.

Execute the hook pass.

Dribbling

The skill of dribbling is used to move the ball up the court. Two types of dribbling will be addressed: the stationary and continuous dribble. You will have to decide which dribble addresses your students' levels of functional ability.

• **Stationary Dribble.** Starting from a stationary position, the student bounces and catches the ball with two hands as they lean to one side. Next they dribble with one hand as they bounce the ball near the main axle of the wheelchair, controlling each bounce with their fingertips. Once they can dribble in a stationary position, they can move forward using an alternating sequence of pushing and dribbling. For example, the student dribbles once then places the ball in the lap; with the ball in the lap, the student pushes the wheelchair twice and repeats the dribble. The student continues down the floor using this alternating dribble, push-push, dribble sequence, each time placing the ball in the lap.

Stationary one-handed dribble: Bounce near the mainwheel.

Stationary one-handed dribble: Fingertip control.

Stationary one-handed dribble: Control the wheelchair.

Forward dribble: Bounce the ball in front of the main axle using fingertip control.

Forward dribble: Dribble, then place the ball in the lap.

Forward dribble: With the ball in the lap, begin pushing the wheelchair.

Forward dribble: Push the wheelchair. Repeat the dribble up the court.

• **Continuous Dribble.** The student bounces the ball ahead of the wheelchair close to the front wheels or casters and quickly moves the hands to the handrims to push the wheelchair. The student continues dribbling the ball forward of the wheelchair while simultaneously pushing the wheelchair down the floor.

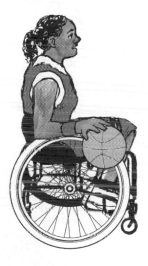

Continuous dribble: Bounce the ball ahead of the wheelchair.

Continuous dribble: Maintain finger-tip control.

Continuous dribble: Continue dribbling while pushing the wheelchair.

Shooting

Students should master the two-handed shot before moving on to the one-handed shot. With a two-handed shot, the student faces the basket with both hands, holding the ball about chest height with elbows flexed and eyes on the target. As the student initiates the shot, emphasize full elbow extension and follow-through with the hands. The

NWBA uses the acronym BEEF, which stands for Balanced position, Elbows flexed, Eyes on target, and Follow through. The BEEF principle works for a one-handed shot also. For a one-handed shot, the student holds the ball in the shooting hand, with the nonshooting hand acting as a support on the opposite side of the ball. Make sure to select a ball that fits the student's hand. The student raises the shooting hand, with elbow and shoulder flexion, to shoulder level and *turns slightly in the wheelchair to create an angle by placing the shooting shoulder slightly closer to the basket*. The student should extend the elbow fully upon release of the ball toward the basket. Use the cue "reach into the cookie jar" as the ball is released to encourage proper wrist flexion and follow-through.

Two-handed shot: Elbows flexed; eyes on target.

Two-handed shot: Full elbow extension upon release.

One-handed shot: Ball is balanced; nonshooting hand supports.

One-handed shot: Turn the shooting shoulder closer to the basket.

One-handed shot: Extend the elbow upon ball release.

One-handed shot: Flex the wrist and "reach into the cookie jar" for follow-through.

Ball Movement

Wheelchair basketball uses many kinds of ball movement similar to those in regulation basketball, including passing, dribbling, and shooting. However, wheelchair basketball has a few ball movement skills that are specific to the game. The following are some of the most important skills that players can add to their repertoires.

• **Bounce Stop.** The bounce stop is used to help the player control their wheelchair while controlling the ball at the same time. The student bounces the ball to the side of the wheelchair in a controlled manner. Beginners should make sure the ball bounces at or above head height. As the student's skill develops, they may work for lower bounces. As the ball bounces up, the student grabs both handrims to stop the wheelchair. The key here is timing the release of the ball and reaching for the handrims of the wheelchair. The student then pulls back with both hands to stop the wheelchair and catches the ball as it rebounds from the floor. Students should be careful to *wrap their fingers around the handrim and not into the spokes* as the wheelchair stops. The student then catches the ball with one hand as the wheelchair stops. As students perfect this skill, they can begin to prepare for the bounce spin.

Bounce stop: Prepare to stop the wheelchair with the opposite hand.

Bounce stop: Bounce the ball slightly above the head and reach for the handrims.

Bounce stop: Stop the wheelchair and catch the ball.

• **Bounce Spin.** The bounce spin is used to elude a defensive player when controlling the ball. The student executes this move by completing a successful bounce stop with a one-handed catch, using the hand on the opposite side of the ball to stop the wheelchair. The hand away from the ball should hold the handrim at 12 o'clock. As the ball hits the floor, the hand on the ball side pulls the handrim backward while the opposite hand pushes forward and down (this will spin the wheelchair). This should be executed as a reciprocal, or "push-pull," movement. As the wheelchair spins 180 degrees, the student's feet will pass under the ball at the apex of the bounce, so the opposite arm should be on the ball side ready to make the catch. Timing is key to this maneuver; students should work on staying in control and spinning while the ball is ascending.

Bounce spin: Bounce the ball near the mainwheel axle. Extend elbow upon ball release.

Bounce spin: Control the wheelchair with the opposite hand.

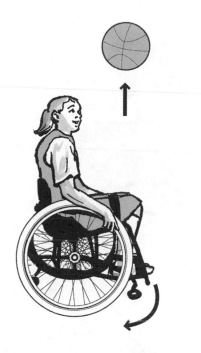

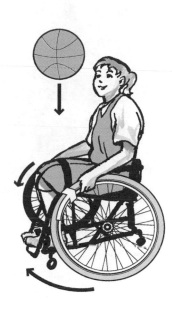

Bounce spin: Bounce the ball above the head; pull the ball-side hand back as the ball rises.

Bounce spin: Execute the push-pull and spin the wheelchair so that the feet pass under the ball.

Bounce spin: Move the wheelchair so that the opposite arm is closer to the ball.

Bounce spin: Catch the ball with the opposite hand.

- **Ball Retrieval.** The ball retrieval is used to recover a loose ball on the court. While the wheelchair is moving, the student approaches a rolled ball from the side and not directly from behind or in front. Once the student is next to the ball and has aligned the mainwheel with the ball, they should lean over and pin the ball against the mainwheel with the hand. As the wheelchair continues to move forward, the mainwheel will roll the pinned ball up from the floor to allow the student to secure it in their lap. To help stabilize themselves during this maneuver, students should hold the opposite side of the wheelchair frame or seat-back posts.

Ball retrieval: Approach the ball from the side and align it with the mainwheel axle.

Ball retrieval: Pin the ball against the mainwheel.

Ball retrieval: Roll the ball up, keeping pressure against the mainwheel.

Ball retrieval: Pull the ball into the lap, position the hands on the rims, and push forward.

Functional Profiles and General Modifications

Not all students with disabilities will be able to execute these skills as described. Since you cannot match activities or skills within activities to all functional levels of your students, you will have to make certain modifications.

Student Functional Profiles

Table 3.2 suggests classifications of student profiles that might fit your teaching situation. These functional profiles are operationally defined using a variation of the classification system employed by the NWBA. You will read similar functional profiles later for indoor wheelchair soccer derived from the National Disability Sports Alliance (NDSA).

Table 3.2	Student Functional Profiles for Wheelchair Basketball
Functional skill level	**Student profile**
Low	Multiple impairments; unable to manually maneuver a wheelchair; needs assistance positioning in wheelchair; needs assistance holding a ball; might use a power wheelchair
Moderate	Able to maneuver a manual wheelchair independently for short distances; can hold a ball independently with two hands; has moderate active range of motion and independent sitting posture
High	Able to maneuver a manual wheelchair independently for longer distances (30-50 ft); can hold a basketball independently with one or two hands; has high active range of motion in upper body and independent sitting posture; can move continuously for 10 minutes without stopping

General Modifications

In table 3.3, you will read how you might apply general modifications for students with disabilities to the six skills necessary to play wheelchair basketball. Notice that these modifications are suggested according to the student functional profiles. You have the choice to decide how to apply these general modifications to your student population.

Table 3.3	General Modifications for Wheelchair Basketball	
Skill level	**Skill**	**Activity modifications**
Low	Passing	Use a small ball.
	Shooting	Drop the ball in a bucket or hoop lying on the floor.
		Throw the ball or beanbag through a suspended hoop placed in front at eye level.
	Dribbling	Knock a ball off a table and have it bounce.
	Bounce stop, Spin	Pull up next to a small Nerf ball placed on a traffic cone. Place small Nerf ball in lap and spin.
	Ball retrieval	Pull up next to a small Nerf ball placed on a traffic cone and reach to retrieve.
Moderate	Passing	Use smaller basketball or volleyball.
	Shooting	Shoot into garbage can. Shoot volleyball or smaller basketball into a lower basketball goal.
	Dribbling	Use two-handed dribble.
	Bounce stop, Spin	No pressure from opponent during a game.
	Ball retrieval	Use a large playground ball instead of a basketball.
High	All skills	No modifications: Used with highest-functioning students.

Game Progressions

The remainder of this chapter presents games you can use with your students with disabilities to teach the various skills described previously. These games are presented in a progression from individual, to small group, to teamwork. Each game is intended to provide you with ideas to help include both students with disabilities and students without disabilities. The individual category is meant for the student with a disability to accomplish with a peer assistant before working in small groups. Small group games can engage two to three students and should include students with and without disabilities. Teamwork games can engage three to five students working together for a single objective. Games for low-functioning students are described first, followed by those for moderate- to high-functioning students.

The games-by-skill-level indexes can be used to determine which games would be appropriate for your students with disabilities, given their levels of function and the skill you are looking to teach. Keep in mind that inclusion means trying to address the three domains of learning in physical education: psychomotor, cognitive, and affective.

Games-by-Skill-Level Index: Low-Functioning Students

Table 3.4 is an index of skills and games for low-functioning students. To read the index, simply find the skill to be addressed and cross-reference it with the game level you desire (individual, small group, or teamwork). This index is followed by game descriptions for low-functioning students. The index and game descriptions for moderate- to high-functioning students follow those for low-functioning students.

Table 3.4	Games-by-Skill-Level Index for Low-Functioning Students—Wheelchair Basketball		
Skills	**Individual activity**	**Small group activity**	**Teamwork**
Passing	Hanging On	Give and Go	Triangle and Go
Shooting	Shot's Away	Pass and Shoot	Triangle and Go
Dribbling	Right Back at You	Pass and Shoot	Triangle and Go
Bounce stop	Gauntlet I	Gauntlet II	Gauntlet III
Bounce spin	Spinning Wheels I	Spinning Wheels II	Spinning Wheels III
Ball retrieval	Reaching Out I	Reaching Out II	Reaching Out III

Game Descriptions

Each game description in this section includes game level, formation, equipment, description, extensions, and inclusion suggestions. Extensions are those instructional ideas that may be used to modify the activity, however slightly, by either increasing or decreasing the level of difficulty as needed. For games that are sequenced, such as Gauntlet I, Gauntlet II, and Gauntlet III, you have the flexibility to start with any game that matches the ability of your students with disabilities and your teaching situation.

You are not bound by the sequence; however, they are written with the idea of moving a student from an individual situation to a teamwork environment.

Skill Passing

◆ Hanging On

Game Level: Individual

Formation: Individual with peer assistant

Equipment: Small Nerf ball, deflated playground ball, Nerf volleyball, or junior basketball

Description: Give the student with a disability the ball and have them hold the ball as long as possible. See how long the student can hold the ball using one hand. Help them with their grasp as needed. If necessary, the student may use two hands.

Extension: Change the position of the hands and arms (for example, in front of the body, over head).

Inclusion Suggestion: The student can demonstrate to the class the ability to accomplish the activity.

◆ Give and Go

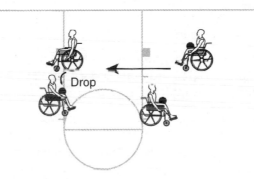

Drop

Game Level: Small group

Formation: Two lines facing each other on opposites sides of the free-throw lane

Equipment: Small Nerf ball, deflated playground ball, Nerf volleyball, or junior basketball

Description: One student has a ball and, on a signal, moves across the lane to their partner. Once next to their partner, they drop the ball on the floor next to their partner. Once the ball hits the floor, another ball is placed in the partner's possession and they must move back across the lane.

Extension: Students without disabilities can alternate being partners.

Inclusion Suggestions: The student with a disability can decide how many times to pass the ball and must indicate that to the class through their own form of communication. The student can also determine who should start the activity.

◆ Triangle and Go

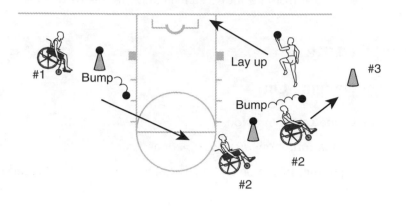

Game Level: Teamwork

Formation: Triangle formation at least 10 feet apart

Equipment: Tall traffic cones, Nerf balls, basketball

Description: Set up three tall traffic cones with large Nerf balls balanced on top of the first two cones. A student with a disability is at each of the first two cones and a student without a disability is at the third cone with a basketball in hand. The object is to have the first student move forward and bump the ball off the cone to simulate a pass. Once the ball is off and rolling, they move to the next cone. The first student continues on to reach the second student. The student at the second cone continues the activity by bumping off the ball and racing to the third cone, where the student without a disability then dribbles toward the basket for a layup. The activity is then repeated.

Extension: Rotate students with disabilities from cones 1 and 2 to cones 2 and 3, and have a student with a disability shoot a shot by dropping the ball into a bucket. The student without a disability moves to the first cone.

Inclusion Suggestions: The student with a disability can keep track of the number of layups made and report to the class for their team. The student can also determine the distance between cones and the distance required for the last person to dribble for the layup.

Skill Shooting

◆ Shot's Away

Game Level: Individual

Formation: Individual with peer assistant

Equipment: Small Nerf ball, deflated playground ball, Nerf volleyball, or junior basketball

Description: The student holds a ball and on command drops it into a bucket or hoop placed next to their wheelchair.

Extension: If grasp and release is an issue, physically assist with the release while verbally cuing the student that the "shot is away" as they release.

Inclusion Suggestions: The student with a disability can determine where to place the bucket or the hoop on the ground. They should attempt to move the target to at least three different locations.

◆ Pass and Shoot

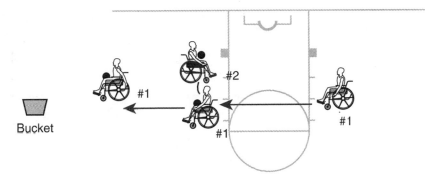

Game Level: Small group

Formation: (Same as Give and Go) Two lines facing each other on opposites sides of the free-throw lane

Equipment: Small Nerf ball, deflated playground ball, Nerf volleyball, or junior basketball; bucket or Hula Hoop

Description: On the signal a student moves across the lane to their partner who places a ball in their lap if the student has the functional ability to do so. The student then continues on to drop the ball into the bucket or hoop placed 10 feet beyond their partner.

Extension: The student without the ball shouts "pass" during the exchange. Place a second bucket beyond the partner, and have the student call out which one to shoot at (that is, left or right).

Inclusion Suggestions: The student who passes the ball can call out or somehow indicate which bucket their partner should shoot at. The student must make the call prior to the partner shooting.

◆ Triangle and Go

Game Level: Teamwork

Formation: Refer to the skill of passing (p. 34).

Equipment: Refer to the skill of passing.

Description: Refer to the skill of passing.

Extension: Challenge each group to complete two complete rotations before shooting the ball. Have each student complete one rotation clockwise, then the second counterclockwise.

Inclusion Suggestions: The student with a disability can assign which student in the group takes the shot, track the number of shots made, or name the group after their favorite basketball team.

Skill Dribbling

◆ Right Back at You

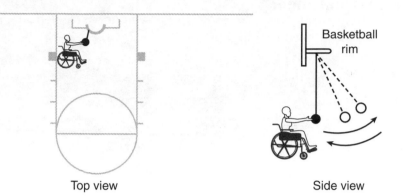

Top view

Side view

Basketball rim

Game Level: Individual

Formation: Individual with peer assistant as needed

Equipment: Elastic band, small rope

Description: Tether a ball to a basketball backboard and allow it to hang at eye level for the student with a disability. The student pushes the ball away and receives it as it returns from the push.

Extension: If grasp and release is an issue, physically assist with emphasis on opening hands to receive the ball.

Inclusion Suggestions: The student with a disability can pick their peer assistant and/or select a favorite basketball team to represent during the game.

◆ Pass and Shoot

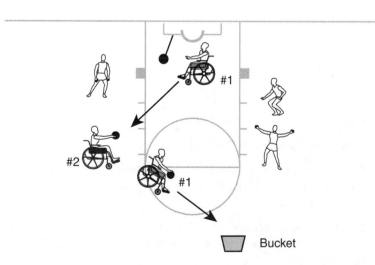

#1

#2

#1

Bucket

Game Level: Small group

Formation: (Same as Shooting) Two lines facing each other on opposites sides of the free-throw lane. The student with a disability is positioned under the basket with the tethered ball.

Equipment: Small Nerf ball, deflated playground ball, Nerf volleyball, or junior basketball; bucket or hula hoop

Description: On a signal the student pushes the ball away to simulate a dribble, then moves down the lane to their partner. Once they reach their partner, a ball is placed in their lap if appropriate, and they continue on to drop it into a bucket or hoop placed 10 feet beyond their partner. (Note: This is the same basic activity as Pass and Shoot with the added tethered ball push.)

Extension: If appropriate, have the student bounce the ball once to the floor after receiving it from their partner and before shooting it into the hoop or bucket.

Inclusion Suggestions: The student with a disability can decide what position each student will start in and what signal to use to begin the activity (for example, a whistle, clap, or shout).

◆ Triangle and Go

Game Level: Teamwork

Formation: Refer to the skill of passing or shooting (p. 34).

Equipment: Refer to the skill of passing or shooting.

Description: Refer to the skill of passing or shooting.

Extension: Challenge each group to complete two rotations before shooting the ball. Have each group complete one rotation clockwise, then the second counterclockwise. Emphasize dribbling from spot to spot.

Inclusion Suggestions: The student with a disability can assign which student in the group takes the shot, track the number of shots made, or name the group after their favorite basketball team. The student could also determine the distance between cones and the distance required for the last person to dribble in for the layup.

Skill Bounce Stop

◆ Gauntlet I

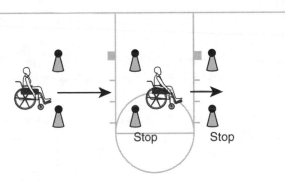

Game Level: Individual

Formation: Individual with peer assistant as needed. Set up two parallel rows of five or six tall traffic cones with approximately six feet between cones. Buckets placed on top of folding chairs will also work. Place a ball or some other object that will balance on top of each of the cones (beanbags work well).

Equipment: Traffic cones, folding chairs, Nerf balls, beanbags

Description: The student is between the rows so that one row is on the student's right and one is on the left. The object is to have the student pass through the gauntlet and be able to stop next to a cone when signaled. To start, the student moves forward as fast as possible through the gauntlet. In response to a random stop signal, the student stops next to the closest cone.

Extension: Once the student has mastered a controlled stop, allow them to pass through, varying their speed and the cone to stop next to, for example, every other cone or every third cone.

Inclusion Suggestions: The student with a disability can decide the pattern of stopping and starting next to a cone. They can also pick the side of the cone to stop next to (left or right), then identify the side of the cone they are on (for example, "I am on the right side").

◆ Gauntlet II

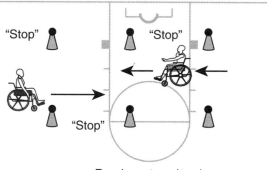

Random stop signals

Game Level: Small group

Formation: Same as Gauntlet I (p. 37)

Equipment: Same as Gauntlet I

Description: Two students move through the activity. Students could be positioned at opposite ends of the gauntlet moving toward each other or facing the same direction in parallel formation.

Extension: If you use a student without a disability as the second student, that student can dribble a basketball while moving. If appropriate, the student with a disability can carry a ball as they move through.

Inclusion Suggestions: The student with a disability can decide the sequence of stopping (for example, every other cone or every third cone). The student can also control the starting and stopping signal as two students without disabilities move through the gauntlet.

◆ Gauntlet III

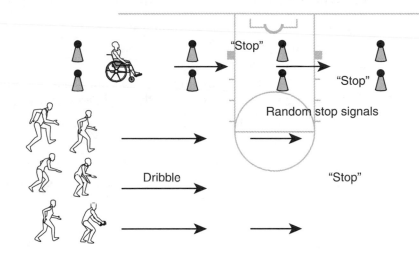

Game Level: Teamwork

Formation: Same as Gauntlet I and II, with an increase to three lines for students without disabilities

Equipment: Same as Gauntlet I and II

Description: Students without disabilities are in three lines next to the gauntlet, each with basketballs ready to dribble, while the student with a disability is positioned in the gauntlet. As the start signal is given, the student with a disability moves forward through the gauntlet, and the students without disabilities move forward dribbling. Each time the stop signal is given, the student with a disability stops at the appropriate cone, while the students without disabilities stop and perform a stationary dribble. The object of the activity is to get all students moving across the floor together as a team.

Extension: The student with a disability changes sides of the gauntlet with each stop (for instance, stop on left, then on right, then on left, and so on).

Inclusion Suggestions: The student with a disability can stop at the cones of their choice, and the entire class must watch them as they move across the floor and stop in unison with them as they continue to move.

Skill Bounce Spin

◆ Spinning Wheels I

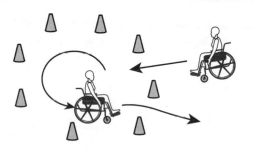

Game Level: Individual

Formation: A circle of traffic cones approximately 10 feet in diameter

Equipment: Traffic cones, basketball, Nerf ball

Description: The student with a disability is about six feet from the circle with a ball secured in their lap. On the signal, the student moves forward into the circle and performs a 360-degree spinning motion within the boundaries of the circle. Once complete, the student moves out of the circle and returns to the starting position.

Extension: Place a single cone on the floor approximately 10 feet from the starting position, and allow the student with a disability to move forward with a ball and complete a 360-degree spin around the cone.

Inclusion Suggestions: The student with a disability can demonstrate this skill to the class. Consider replacing the circle of cones with a circle of classmates, and encourage students to reinforce performance.

◆ Spinning Wheels II

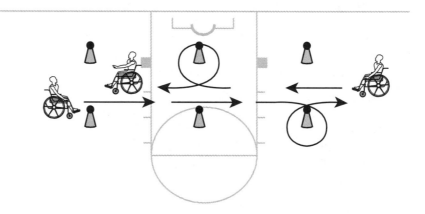

Game Level: Small group

Formation: Same as Gauntlet II (p. 38)

Equipment: Cones, basketball, Nerf balls

Description: Using the formation from Gauntlet II, the students move through the gauntlet, stopping at the designated cone as described earlier. This time, when the student stops at the cone, they must spin their wheelchair around the cone once before continuing on to the next cone. If two students have started on opposite ends of the gauntlet, make sure to allow enough room for circling the cones.

Extension: Replace cones in the gauntlet with students from the class.

Inclusion Suggestion: The student with a disability can predict (if appropriate) how much time it will take to complete the gauntlet for Spinning Wheels II.

◆ Spinning Wheels III

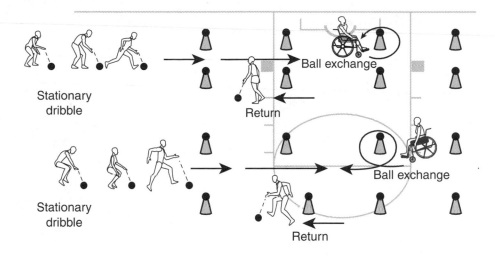

Game Level: Teamwork

Formation: Same as Gauntlet I. Create two teams, each with students with and without disabilities ready to race each through their own gauntlet.

Equipment: Same as Spinning Wheels I and II

Description: Equally divide the students with disabilities on each team, and place them in the gauntlet next to a designated cone. Students without disabilities form a line ready to dribble through the gauntlet. Each student waiting in line must have a ball. On the signal, the first student dribbles to the student with a disability and places the ball in their lap. Once the ball is secured, the student spins around their cone once and returns the ball to the first student. The student without a disability retrieves the ball and dribbles back to the starting line, where the next student repeats the movement. While the first student is moving through the gauntlet, the remaining students are performing a stationary dribble while waiting their turn. The activity is over when the last student passes through the gauntlet.

Extension: Increase or decrease the distance to the first student with a disability according to the skill level of the students without disabilities. Repeat the activity, having the students without disabilities use the nondominant hand.

Inclusion Suggestion: The student with a disability can determine the order of rotation for their team; that is, they can decide who gets to go first, second, and so on.

Skill Ball Retrieval

◆ Reaching Out I

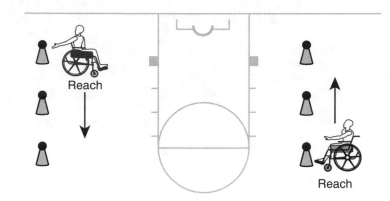

Game Level: Individual

Formation: Set up a row of five or six tall traffic cones or folding chairs approximately six feet apart. Place a ball or some other object that will balance on top of the cones or folding chairs (beanbags work well).

Equipment: Traffic cones, folding chairs, beanbags, Nerf ball

Description: The student with a disability is next to the cones or chairs and reaches to the side in an attempt to retrieve or touch the object, depending on functional level.

Extension: Make sure to work both right- and left-side retrieval skills.

Inclusion Suggestion: Replace cones with students without disabilities.

◆ Reaching Out II

Game Level: Small group

Formation: Place two long benches in parallel formation wide enough to support a playground ball placed in the space created by the two benches without falling through.

Equipment: Cones, basketball, Nerf balls, long benches or folding tables

Description: A student without a disability is at one end of the benches ready to roll the ball forward. A student with a disability is next to the benches, ready to move forward. On a signal, the student without a disability rolls the ball forward down the benches while the student with a disability also moves forward and attempts to stop the ball before it reaches the other end.

Extension: Repeat for the right- and left-side retrieval skills.

Inclusion Suggestions: The student with a disability can initiate rolling the ball to be retrieved by the student without a disability. The student with a disability can also decide how many times they must complete the activity before rotating out of the activity.

◆ **Reaching Out III**

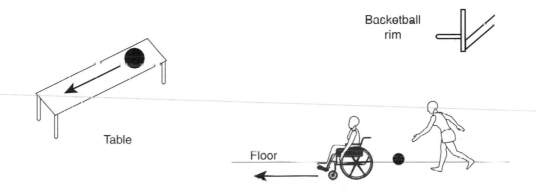

Game Level: Teamwork

Formation: Same as Reaching Out II

Equipment: Same as Reaching Out II

Description: Same as Reaching Out II, with noted extension suggestions

Extension: This time remove the benches and roll the ball on a long folding table or on the floor. When rolling on a table, make sure to allow enough room for the student with a disability to move next to the table safely, and try to use a ball that rolls with more control, such as a slightly deflated basketball, soccer ball, or playground ball.

Inclusion Suggestions: The student with a disability can determine the distance the ball should be rolled when using the floor for retrieval. The student can also determine the number of times each team should retrieve the ball before changing positions.

Games-by-Skill-Level Index: Moderate- to High-Functioning Students

The index in table 3.5 is designed to address those students with disabilities who are considered to have moderate to high functional ability. The progression of activity suggestions remains the same, from individual, to small group, to teamwork.

Table 3.5	Games-by-Skill-Level Index for Moderate- to High-Functioning Students—Wheelchair Basketball		
Skills	Individual activity	Small group activity	Teamwork
Passing	Target Toss	Remember Me	Call It Out
Shooting	Spinning the Ball	In the Bucket	At the Hoop
Dribbling	Stationary	On the Move I	On the Move II
Bounce stop	Stop the Music I	Stop the Music II	Stop the Music III
Bounce spin	Crossover	Spin City I	Spin City II
Ball retrieval	Reach for It	Down and Back	Giddy Up

Game Descriptions

Eighteen games designed for moderate- to high-functioning students are described in the following section. Modify these games as needed for your teaching situation.

Skill Passing (for Chest, Bounce, Hook)

◆ Target Toss

Chest pass Bounce pass

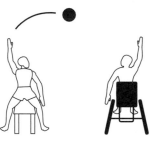

Hook pass

Game Level: Individual

Formation: Individual with peer assistant

Equipment: Basketball, targets for wall, cones for distance markers

Description: Position a student with the ball, making sure to review each of the key points for executing the chest, bounce, and hook passes. For the chest pass, place a target on the wall (e.g., a two-foot-diameter circle) and have the student with a disability pass the ball into the target from a distance of three to four feet. For the bounce pass, position a partner about six to eight feet away facing the student with the ball. Review the cues for the bounce pass and have the partners pass back and forth. For the hook pass, use the same position as the bounce pass, except turn the partners sideways so that each player's dominant side is away from the partner before performing the pass.

Extensions: For the bounce pass have a student without a disability sit on a bench or in a folding chair. For the hook pass, higher-skilled students can try passing with the nondominant hand.

Inclusion Suggestions: The student with a disability can demonstrate to the class their ability to accomplish the activity and determine three new distances for the target. The student can also determine two additional skills to be added to this activity. Use students without disabilities as assistants for retrieving and providing appropriate feedback.

◆ Remember Me

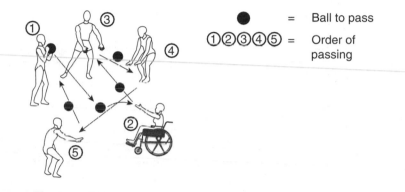

Game Level: Small group

Formation: Position students with and without disabilities in a small circle with one basketball per circle.

Equipment: Basketball, Nerf ball, or Nerf volleyball

Description: On a signal the students use a chest pass to move the ball back and forth across and around the circle. The object of the activity is to pass the ball around the circle in the same sequence as the original pattern, meaning that once the ball has been passed around the circle and everyone has touched it, the second time around should follow the same pattern with students passing to the same individuals each time.

Extensions: Change the type of pass used. For example, for the first two trips students can use the chest pass, for the next two the bounce pass, and so on. For students who have difficulty catching a basketball, change the type of ball or change the distance needed to pass for success.

Inclusion Suggestion: Students with disabilities can determine the sequence of passes (for example, chest to bounce or bounce to hook).

◆ Call It Out

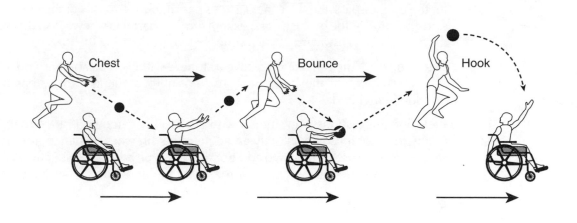

Game Level: Teamwork

Formation: Students are in parallel line formation opposite a partner. This is a dynamic formation with students moving forward in pairs as they pass the ball. Students with and without disabilities should be paired up.

Equipment: Basketball, playground ball, or Nerf ball

Description: Each set of partners has a basketball and on the signal must move forward across the floor, passing the ball as they move. Students must stay about 15 to 20 feet apart and keep the ball ahead of their partner. The teacher changes the type of pass every two or three trips down the floor by calling out a new pass—for example, chest pass, bounce pass, hook pass. The objective is to get one trip complete without a miss using each of the passes presented.

Extension: For students with varying degrees of manual wheelchair propulsion, consider changing the type of ball used to pass and/or the distance passed.

Inclusion Suggestion: The student with a disability can call out the pass to be executed.

Skill Shooting

◆ Spinning the Ball

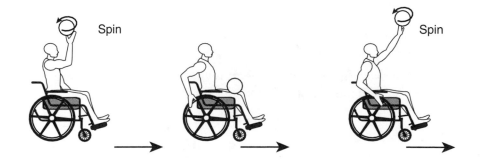

Game Level: Individual

Formation: Individual with peer assistant as needed

Equipment: Basketball, playground ball, or Nerf volleyball

Description: The purpose of this activity is to allow the student with moderate functional ability to practice ball release when shooting a basketball. Using the key teaching points presented earlier, have the student balance a basketball in the shooting hand with the shooting arm up overhead. From this position, have the student flex the elbow and wrist while releasing the ball from the hand and putting a rotation or spin on the ball. Emphasize spinning the ball upon release with the cue of "reach into the cookie jar."

Extension: Change the size of the ball if the student is unable to control a basketball. Other choices might include a Nerf volleyball or a soccer ball.

Inclusion Suggestions: The student with a disability can demonstrate their skill level, if appropriate, or teach a small group of students without disabilities the key teaching points.

◆ In the Bucket

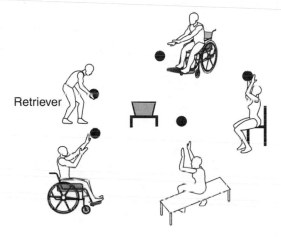

Retriever

Game Level: Small group

Formation: Position students with and without disabilities in a small circle, each with a basketball. Place a plastic garbage can or large barrel on a small table in the center of the circle approximately four to six feet from the students.

Equipment: Basketball, table, chair, bucket, garbage can

Description: On a signal students practice their shooting skills into the garbage can or barrel. Designate one student to retrieve the balls from the bucket and have students without disabilities use a folding chair or bench to shoot from a seated position.

Extension: Vary the height of the garbage can or barrel by placing it either on the floor, on a small table, or on the stage or a volleyball referee's stand.

Inclusion Suggestions: The student with a disability can report to the teacher the path of the shot (for example, short or long, left or right). The student can also select which type of ball to shoot for the group.

◆ At the Hoop

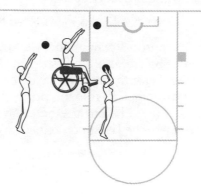

Game Level: Teamwork

Formation: Position students with and without disabilities approximately three feet from a regulation basketball backboard and rim.

Equipment: Basketball, regulation backboard and rim

Description: Students shoot at the hoop using the teaching points presented. Teamwork can be accomplished by playing several games such as HORSE or Around the World. Teamwork can also be accomplished by combining games such as At the Hoop and Call It Out.

Extension: Students with and without disabilities could form teams that shoot at the basket, rebound the ball, and move down the court to the opposite basket while practicing passing.

Inclusion Suggestion: The student with a disability can create one alternative to this activity and present it to the group.

Skill Dribbling

◆ Stationary

Game Level: Individual

Formation: Individual with peer assistant as needed

Equipment: Basketball, 10-inch playground ball, folding chairs, benches

Description: The purpose of this activity is to allow the student with moderate or high functional ability to practice dribbling the ball in a stationary position.

Extensions: Students with less functional ability could start with a two-handed bounce and catch while leaning to the side of the wheelchair. Also, students who have difficulty controlling a regulation basketball could use a larger playground ball. Students without disabilities could be included in this activity by placing folding chairs or benches in the same area and having them participate from a seated position.

Inclusion Suggestion: The student with a disability could decide a set number of successful dribbles to accomplish before changing hands (for example, 10 with the right hand and then 10 with the left).

◆ On the Move I

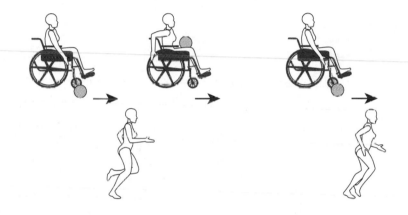

Game Level: Small group

Formation: The student with a disability is partnered with a student without a disability in a side-by-side formation, facing the same direction and ready to move across the gym floor.

Equipment: Basketball or 10-inch playground ball, folding chairs, benches

Description: The student with a disability pushes forward in their wheelchair while carrying the ball in their lap. Once they are moving, they dribble using one hand while controlling their wheelchair. They can return the ball to their lap after traveling 15 feet. A student without a disability walks next to the wheelchair to help with errant dribbling. Continue the activity across the gymnasium floor. On the return trip, the student without a disability performs the dribble using proper techniques, and the student with a disability serves as the assistant to recover errant dribbles.

Extension: Increase the difficulty of this activity by placing traffic cones in a line about six to eight feet apart, and instruct the students to dribble in a weave pattern in and out among the cones.

Inclusion Suggestions: A student without a disability performs the dribble in both directions while the student with a disability critiques their movement. At the end of both trips across the gym, the student with a disability shares what aspects look correct and which movements need work. The two students then reverse rolls and repeat the activity.

◆ On the Move II

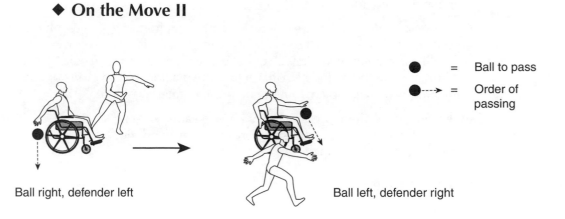

Ball right, defender left   Ball left, defender right

● = Ball to pass

●--→ = Order of passing

Game Level: Teamwork

Formation: Same position as On the Move I

Equipment: Basketball or 10-inch playground ball, folding chairs, benches

Description: With this activity the student without a disability challenges the dribble by representing a defender and changing positions next to the wheelchair. With each attempt at dribbling, the student with a disability must keep the ball on the opposite side of the wheelchair away from the defender. That is, as the student with a disability dribbles the ball on the right side, the defender should be on the left; and as the defender switches to the other side, so should the dribble. Once the students become efficient, you might consider some form of relay activity.

Extension: Try this activity in a stationary formation before moving across the gym floor.

Inclusion Suggestions: The student with a disability can decide who starts first with the ball. The student can also count successful switches from side to side and report the count to the teacher.

Skill Bounce Stop

◆ Stop the Music I

Game Level: Individual

Formation: The purpose of this activity is to allow the students to move in progression of skill development, working from individual, to small group, to teamwork. The basic concept of Stop the Music is to allow students to move freely or in an organized pattern while dribbling the basketball with the music playing. Once the music stops, the students should perform a bounce stop using the cues provided earlier.

Equipment: Basketball, 10-inch playground ball, cones

Description: Students with and without disabilities each have a ball to dribble. On a signal, the student with a disability moves about the gymnasium, performing a lap or push dribble. The teacher randomly stops the music. When the music stops, all students perform the bounce stop as instructed. Students without disabilities would pick up their dribble and assume a basic basketball position with slight bend at waist, knees bent, weight evenly distributed, and eyes forward.

Extension: Students with less functional ability could start with the two-handed bounce and catch while leaning to the side of the wheelchair.

Inclusion Suggestion: The student with a disability can decide a set number of successful dribbles to accomplish before changing hands (for example, 10 with the right hand, then 10 with the left).

◆ Stop the Music II

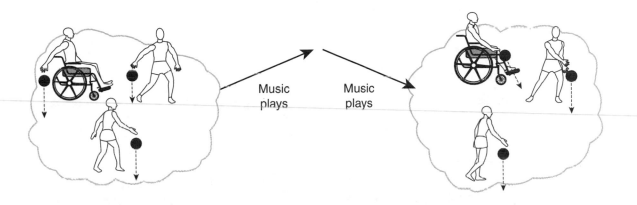

Music plays   Music plays

Game Level: Small group

Formation: Performed as in Stop the Music I; however, this time students are in small groups positioned around the gymnasium.

Equipment: Basketball or 10-inch playground ball, music player

Description: The objective of the activity is to get the small group to travel together around the gymnasium while dribbling the basketball to the music. Once the music stops, the students should perform a bounce stop or assume a basic basketball ready position.

Extension: Increase the difficulty with this activity by placing traffic cones around the gym to be avoided by the groups.

Inclusion Suggestion: The student with a disability can call out or somehow indicate which hand to dribble with (for example, "right-hand dribble, now switch to left").

◆ Stop the Music III

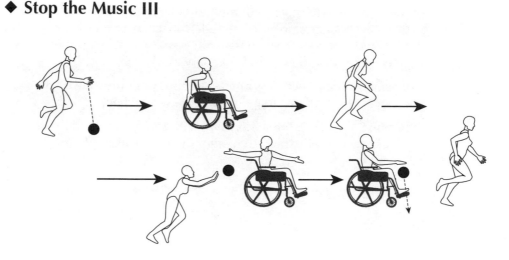

Game Level: Teamwork

Formation: Form two or three lines (depending on the size of the class) trying to alternate a student with a disability and a student without a disability within each line. Spread the lines out so that there is about 10 feet between each student and all students are facing the same direction.

Equipment: Basketball or 10-inch playground ball, music player

Description: Place one basketball at the beginning of each line. The objective of the activity is to have each student move forward dribbling the ball until they reach the student in front of them. Once they reach the student in front of them, they must perform a bounce stop under control, then pass it to their teammate, who continues on to the next teammate. If the music stops before they reach a teammate, they must react and perform the bounce stop wherever they are in the activity. As the music continues, so should the activity.

Extensions: Increase or decrease the distance between teammates. Play music with varying tempos.

Inclusion Suggestion: The student with a disability can select the music to be played.

Skill Bounce Spin

◆ Crossover

Game Level: Individual

Formation: The student can work alone using a peer to help retrieve the missed played balls.

Equipment: Basketball, 10-inch playground ball, cones

Description: Use all the cues suggested earlier in this chapter for the bounce spin (pages 28 to 29). Allow students with less function to use two hands during the bounce and catch phase of the skill. Students without disabilities could be positioned next to the student with a disability to help with errant bounce spins.

Extension: Allow students without disabilities to perform the crossover dribble maneuver used in regulation basketball. Students with less functional ability could start with the two-handed bounce and catch while leaning to the side of the wheelchair.

Inclusion Suggestion: The student with a disability can decide a set number of successful bounce spins or crossover dribbles to be accomplished by the class.

◆ Spin City I

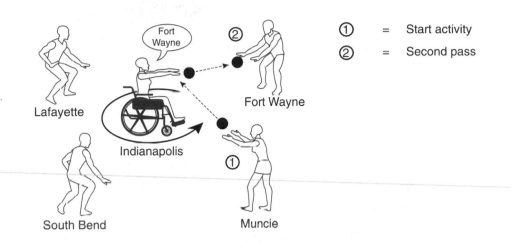

Game Level: Small group

Formation: Students in small circle formations around the gymnasium with one student in the middle

Equipment: Basketball or 10-inch playground ball

Description: Each circle represents a state within the United States (for example, Indiana). Each member of the circle represents a city in the state (for example, Muncie), and the person in the middle represents the capital of the state (for example, Indianapolis). Place a ball with any city within the state and have that person pass the ball to the capital. Once the person in the middle catches the ball, they must perform a bounce spin and pass the ball to a new city. As they pass the ball to a new city, they must call the name of the city out loud before passing it. As the new city catches the ball, they must in turn perform a bounce spin and pass it back to the capital. The activity continues until all cities have been called. Students without disabilities should perform a crossover dribble or another skill selected by the teacher.

Extension: Change the theme of the activity to use the names of universities within states or the names of automobiles within manufacturers.

Inclusion Suggestion: The student with a disability can select the new category (for example, cars, planes, boats, and so on).

◆ Spin City II

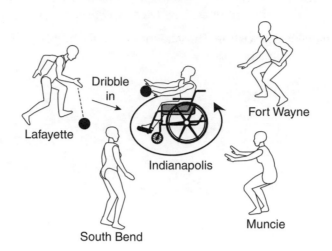

Game Level: Teamwork

Formation: Same formation as Spin City I

Equipment: Basketball or 10-inch playground ball, music player

Description: Same as Spin City I except that students get the ball to the capital by dribbling into the center instead of passing it in. The bounce spin is still performed by the individual receiving the ball.

Extension: To create more of a teamwork emphasis, increase the number of balls per state and allow any city to move forward in random order rather than sequentially around the circle. Increase or decrease the distance between teammates.

Inclusion Suggestion: The student with a disability can determine which hand everyone should be dribbling with.

Skill Ball Retrieval

◆ Reach for It

Game Level: Individual

Formation: Individual with peer assistant as needed

Equipment: Basketball or 10-inch playground ball

Description: Place a ball next to the mainwheel of the wheelchair and have the student shift their weight to the side the ball is on, support the shift with the opposite arm, and lean over to reach for the ball. Once they have the ball under control, they should initiate a small push with the opposite arm to move the wheelchair forward while pressing the ball against the mainwheel of the wheelchair. As the wheel turns forward, it should bring the ball up to the student's lap for retrieval.

Extension: The student should practice this using both the left and right side for retrieval.

Inclusion Suggestion: The student can demonstrate their skills to the class when appropriate.

◆ Down and Back

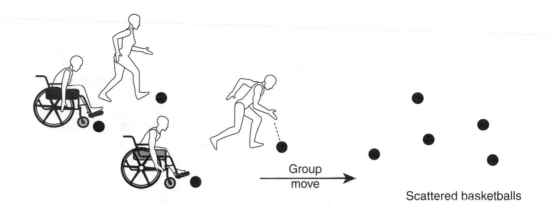

Group move

Scattered basketballs

Game Level: Small group

Formation: Students with and without disabilities work together in this activity. Place students in small groups scattered around the gymnasium.

Equipment: Basketballs, playground balls, or Nerf volleyballs

Description: Place as many basketballs or other balls as possible on the floor around the gymnasium. Try to have enough for each student. On a signal, students move as a group to the basketballs. Once they have retrieved a ball, they move as a group to reposition the basketballs by dribbling to a new location. Emphasis is on ball retrieval. Once the group has moved to a new location, they must place the ball on the ground and be ready to repeat the activity. Groups must move at least 10 feet to a new location.

Extension: Change the distance between groups or between placement of the basketballs.

Inclusion Suggestion: The student with a disability can determine the new location of movement.

◆ Giddy Up

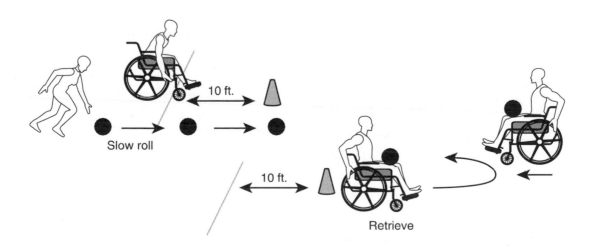

10 ft.

Slow roll

10 ft.

Retrieve

Game Level: Teamwork

Formation: Students are in line formation. Try to alternate a student with a disability with a student without a disability in each line.

Equipment: Basketball or 10-inch playground ball, cones

Description: Place a basketball with the second person in line and instruct them to roll the ball forward, *slowly*, at the start signal. Place a cone about 10 feet in front of each line to serve as a target for the person rolling the ball. The objective of the activity is to have the first person in line retrieve the ball once it has passed the cone. The retriever cannot move until the ball has passed the cone. Once the ball has been retrieved, that person returns it to their team, passing it to the second person in line. Once the second person has the ball, the activity is repeated. Continue until all students have been a roller and a retriever.

Extensions: Change the size of the ball, the weight of the ball, or the distance to the cone. Students with limited mobility might be positioned in the retrieval position and have the ball rolled to them, thus eliminating the mobility component.

Inclusion Suggestion: The student with a disability can determine the order of performance for their team.

chapter

4

Indoor Wheelchair Soccer

Indoor wheelchair soccer is a sport that is sanctioned by the National Disability Sports Alliance (NDSA). Each year for the past 12 years, more than 10 teams from around the United States have traveled to play in national competition. Each team carries approximately 15 players, plus coaches and managers. The national tournament has been hosted in Houston, Texas; San Diego, California; Atlanta, Georgia; Springfield, Massachusetts; and New London, Connecticut. Although this sport is traditionally played by individuals with cerebral palsy, individuals with spinal cord injuries, amputations, or conditions considered as *les autres* (the others; e.g., muscular dystrophy and multiple sclerosis) are eligible to play.

Description of the Sport

Indoor wheelchair soccer, which is similar to traditional outdoor soccer, with some rules modified from indoor team handball, dates back to the early 1980s. This sport has been hotly contested at the international and national levels. At the time of this writing, national competition had taken precedence by offering regional and national tournaments. Although there are over 16 pages of rules authored by the NDSA, only those rules considered essential to the game will be presented here.

Field of Play

The game is played on a court the size of a high school basketball court, using a 10-inch yellow playground ball. You will be limited to the space available in your school's facility, so feel free to modify as needed.

Players

There are two teams of no more than six and no fewer than four players. Each team is allowed one goalkeeper. Formerly, the game had nine players on each team, with two goalkeepers. The number of players on the floor will depend on your facility and class size; use whatever works best for you.

Equipment

The official ball is a 10-inch yellow playground ball. You may, however, use whatever ball works best for your situation. Other types of balls that may be used include beach balls and large cage balls.

Starting the Game

The game is started with a kickoff at center court. The teams are lined up facing each other about 15 feet apart and remain stationary until the ball has been moved by an offensive player one complete circumference (i.e., a pass to a teammate). If 15 feet is not available, allow enough distance for a suitable kickoff procedure.

Game Objective

Once the game has been started, the objective is to get the ball completely into the opponents' net, just as in outdoor soccer. The majority of ball movement is performed by throwing and catching; however, players who cannot throw and catch are allowed to use the lower extremities to move the ball. Therefore, a goal may be scored by throwing or kicking the ball completely into the opponents' goal. The goals in an official game are made of plastic or metal and stand five feet six inches high and five feet wide, with a three-foot depth. In your physical education class you may mark an area of compatible goal width using folding chairs or gymnastics mats.

As play continues, each team tries to maneuver up and down the court, passing the ball into position to shoot at the goal. Once a player has control of the ball, they have three seconds to pass, dribble, or shoot. A player may move the ball up the court using a continuous dribble, or they may dribble once, place the ball in their lap, and push their wheelchair forward without dribbling. If they use this latter form of ball movement, they must dribble again or pass the ball within three seconds of the time they place the ball in their lap. The three-second infraction results in a side-out, or turnover.

The ball is always considered to be in play. It must go completely past a sideline or end line to be considered out of bounds. If a ball is ruled out of bounds, the player in-bounding the ball must use a two-handed overhead throwing motion to return the ball

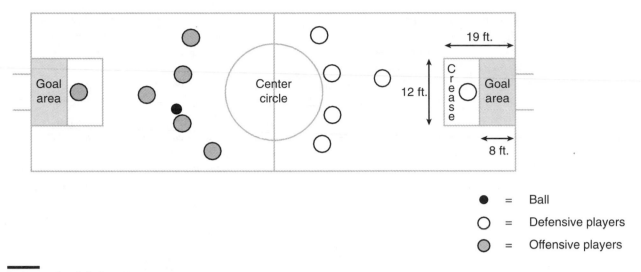

Indoor wheelchair soccer court.

to play. The player has five seconds to in-bound the ball, and all defensive and offensive players must allow that player a three-foot area during the throw. If the ball is in-bounded and travels across the court without being touched by another player, the ball is returned to the in-bounding site and awarded as a turnover to be in-bounded by the opponent. A goal cannot be scored off a direct in-bound play without the ball touching another player.

Goals may be scored from anywhere on the court but cannot be scored from beyond the midcourt line. Goals are not allowed if they are the result of a direct kick from a kickoff play or a sideline throw-in without touching another offensive or defensive player. Goals count as one point. The goal area directly in front of the net cannot be penetrated by either the offensive or defensive team. This area should be considered similar to the crease area in hockey, which means the only players allowed in this area are the goalies for each team. The goal area is marked by an 8 foot-deep and 12-foot-wide area using the basketball end line under the basket and the free-throw lane lines. See the court diagram in figure 4.1 for specific details.

Game Length

Official games are 50 minutes in length, with two 25-minute halves and a 15-minute interval between halves. Obviously, the length of time will be dictated by the time available in your schedule. Each team is allowed two time-outs per half, but again, you may create any rule that fits your program needs.

General Rules/Penalties

Penalties in the game result in a penalty shot. During the penalty shot, all players except the shooter and the defensive goalkeeper must line up at the center court line. Offensive players will be allowed outside positions, and defensive players will be allowed inside positions at center court. All players must remain in a stationary position until the ball is in play or the penalty shot has been taken. If a defensive player violates the rules during a penalty shot, the shot is retaken. If an offensive player commits a violation during the penalty shot, a side-out, or throw-in, is awarded. Once the ball leaves the player's possession and travels one circumference, it is considered in play and all players may move. If the ball alludes the goalie and results in a score, play is stopped and started again at center court with a new kickoff. If the penalty shot attempt is blocked and bounces back into the playing area, it is considered playable immediately. However, if the penalty shot attempt is blocked and secured by the goalie (i.e., held for five seconds), the goalie has three options: pass the ball back into play, take the ball into play by dribbling out of the goal area, or hold the ball and be awarded a throw-in by the referee.

Several violations will result in a penalty shot. Again, for the ease of implementing the game in your program, two basic infractions are recommended to be enforced. A penalty should be called if a player does not maintain control of their wheelchair, which results in "ramming" another player. A second infraction that should be enforced is grabbing an opponent during a shot on goal. Indoor wheelchair soccer can be an aggressive game. Because players are allowed to reach and grab for the ball as it is moved up and down the court, you will need to develop a set of safety rules specific to your situation.

Finally, indoor wheelchair soccer has a system of time penalties similar to those in soccer, using a series of colored cards indicating the severity of the infraction. Blue cards are for all personal fouls, team time penalties, and poor sporting behavior. Yellow cards are used as a warning that a player's next penalty will result in ejection, and red cards are used for ejection. Each violation results in players receiving timed penalties in the penalty box area as in soccer (e.g., player misconduct gets two minutes, poor sporting behavior gets two minutes).

Remember that in a physical education class you are trying to increase playing time and participation. Although it is important to ensure that your students are safe, an overemphasis of rules and infractions will take playing time away from your class members.

Summary of the Sport

Table 4.1 provides an overview of indoor wheelchair soccer. This quick reference will help you learn how to play the game.

Table 4.1	Overview of Indoor Wheelchair Soccer
Field of play	Basketball court: 50 ft by 94 ft and no larger than 50 ft by 100 ft
	Goal area: 12 ft wide by 8 ft deep
	Goals: 5 ft wide and 5 ft 6 in. high (can be made from wood, plastic, or metal)
	Penalty shot line: 19 ft from the basketball end line in front of the goal (this is usually the same free-throw line in basketball).
Players	Maximum allowed on court is six players.
Equipment	10-in. yellow playground ball inflated to 2 psi.
	All players must play in wheelchairs. Motorized scooters are not allowed in an official competition.
	Foot platform heights, at the forward point, cannot be more than 4-3/4 in. from the floor.
	All wheelchairs must have straps extending from one side of the chair to the other, behind the players legs, 6 in. above the platforms.
Legal start	A legal start is conducted when an offensive player takes the ball inside the center circle and moves it the distance of its own circumference in a direction parallel to or behind the center line. At least one player must touch the ball before a goal can be scored.

If an offensive player commits a violation prior to the kicker's initial movement, the kickoff is awarded to the opposing team. If the defense commits a violation, the kickoff is repeated.

Ball in play	The ball is in play at all times—when rebounding off a goalpost or the referee, or until the referee blows the whistle.
	The ball is out of play when it completely crosses over the sideline or end line, or when it makes contact with a building structure above the area of play.
	A two-handed behind-the-head (overhead) throw is used to put the ball in play from a throw-in. If a player cannot use both hands, they must attempt the overhead throw using one.
	If the ball is not in-bounded within 5 sec, a turnover is awarded.
	The ball must travel completely over the line to be considered out of bounds. If a player is struck by a ball while they are out of bounds, there is no change of possession.
	Defensive players may not interfere with the in-bounding player's reentry to the court.
	In-bounding must be accomplished through the air; if the ball bounces on the line, it will be awarded to the other team at the same location.
Ball movement	A player may use hands, feet, chair, or any part of their body to move the ball.
	A player may dribble the ball with one or two hands.
	A player has 3 sec to pass, dribble, or shoot once they have gained possession of the ball.
	A player may not touch the playing surface while in possession of the ball. Only those players who use their feet to propel the wheelchair will be exempt.
	Goalkeepers may leave the goal area when they are in possession of the ball but are then considered as a player on the court and have 3 sec to pass, dribble, or shoot.
Goal area play	If the ball is in the goal area, other players may try to gain possession. They must avoid (a) touching any part of the goal area with their wheelchair or body or (b) physically interfering with the goalkeeper.
	If an offensive player violates either (a) or (b), the result is a side-out for the other team.
	If a defensive player violates either (a) or (b), the result is a penalty shot for the other team.
Goal scored	A goal is scored when the entire ball passes through the plane of the goal line. A goalkeeper can stop a ball halfway through the plane of the goal and hold it stationary for 5 sec, resulting in a throw-in for their team.
Penalty shots	All players are at center court, with offensive players on the outside and defensive players on the inside. Shooter takes the shot from the free-throw line with only the goalkeeper defending.
	No player may move until the ball is considered in play (moves one complete circumference).
	If an offensive player moves before the shot, the ball is awarded to the defense on a side-out.
	If the defensive player moves before the shot, the penalty shot is retaken. If the penalty shot is made, no violations are considered.

(continued)

Table 4.1	(continued)
Blocking versus ramming	Blocking is a legal move and is defined by any player positioning their wheelchair to impede another player's movement. The player must have established position first. Ramming is an illegal move defined as a collision from any angle in which a player fails to gain position first or fails to control their own wheelchair. Players are expected to maintain control of their wheelchairs at all times.
Loss of possession	The following result in loss of possession to the victimized team: • Offensive player enters the goal area to gain an advantage. • Player touches the floor while in possession of the ball. • Offensive player considered ramming another player. • Player covers the ball with the wheelchair for more than three seconds. • Goalkeeper gains possession of the ball in the play area and carries it back into the goal area.
Penalty shots awarded	Defensive player rams an opponent in a scoring attempt. Any player holds or hooks an opponent's wheelchair or body. Defensive player enters the goal area during an attempt to score. Defensive player pushes an offensive player into the goal area.

Skills to Be Taught

In this section you will learn how to teach the five basic skills necessary to play indoor wheelchair soccer. These skills can be taught in your physical education class to students with and without disabilities. Notice that within passing/shooting there are three variations: two-handed, bounce, and baseball. You will have to decide which skills will be appropriate for your students.

Passing

Indoor wheelchair soccer uses three types of passes. Passing is used to move the ball up and down the court in an attempt to invade the opponent's territory. Passing is used to position players to shoot at the goal. The types of passes used in this sport are similar to the passes discussed in wheelchair basketball.

- **Two-Handed Pass.** The student places the hands on each side of the ball and draws the ball into the chest by flexing the elbows, then extends the elbows forcefully to pass the ball to a teammate. This is similar to the chest pass in wheelchair basketball.

Preparation for two-handed chest pass.

Execution of two-handed chest pass.

• **Bounce Pass.** This pass uses the same mechanics as that of the two-handed pass with the following emphasis: the student tries to land the ball in the receiver's lap by bouncing it on the floor between them.

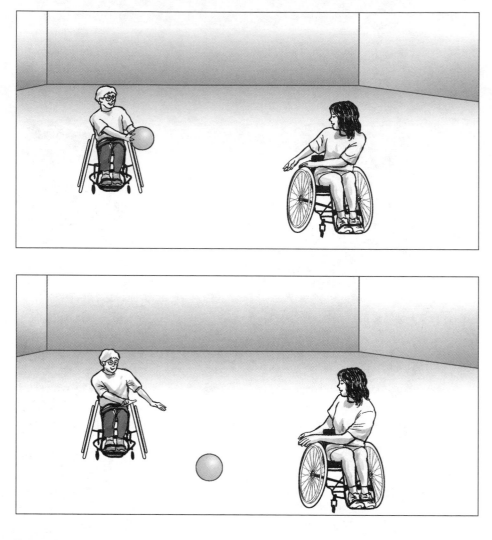

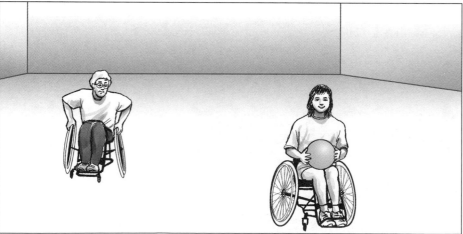

Bounce ball into partner's lap.

- **Baseball Pass.** This pass is used to move the ball up the floor in a hurry or to shoot a goal. The student stabilizes and balances the trunk in the wheelchair while bringing the ball back and up to a "baseball" throwing position. Then the student raises the ball under control, moves it up and forward, maintains balance upon release, and follows through.

Position ball in baseball throwing position.

Move ball forward.

Release and follow through.

Dribbling

The skill of dribbling is used to move the ball up the court. Only the push dribble will be discussed for soccer because the lap dribble from basketball might encourage a violation of the three-second rule discussed earlier.

- **Push Dribble.** The student bounces the ball ahead of the wheelchair closer to the front wheels, or casters. As the ball is pushed ahead, the student moves the hands quickly to the handrims and wheels to push the wheelchair. The student then continues dribbling the ball forward of the wheelchair while simultaneously pushing the wheelchair down the floor.

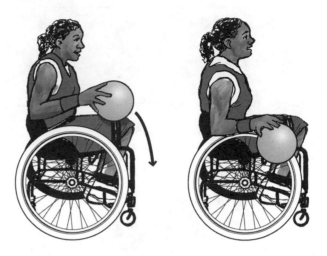

Bounce the ball ahead of the wheelchair.

Continue dribbling up the floor.

Throw-In

The throw-in is used to place the ball in play after a turnover or an out-of-bounds call by the referee. The throw-in must be performed with a two-handed overhead motion if possible.

While maintaining a balanced sitting position and facing the court, the student grips the ball with two hands as in the two-handed chest pass. Maintaining balance, the

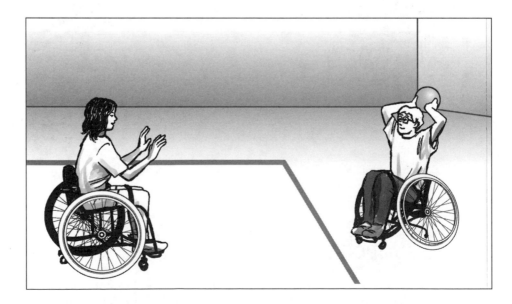

Raise ball overhead with two hands.

student raises the ball up with both hands over and behind the head. Once the ball is completely behind the head, the student pulls both hands forward to release the ball. The student should be sure to extend the elbow upon release of the ball toward the court with full range of motion and follow through upon release.

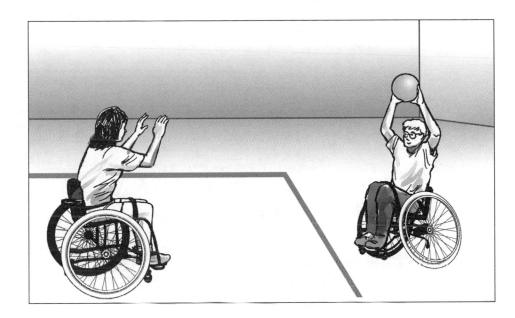

Pull ball forward overhead.

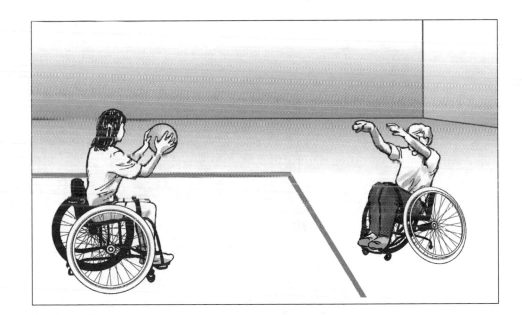

Release and follow through.

Blocking

This is a key position for the defense. Students without disabilities can play this position in your included setting by blocking with their nondominant hand or arm.

• **Goalkeeper Block.** Positioned in front of the attacker, the student's hands are on the rims ready to move the wheelchair as needed to reduce the angle of the shot (forward, backward, left, or right). The goalie should maintain a balanced position, sitting as tall as possible. As the shot is taken, the student extends the arms upward and minimizes the space between the arms to help protect the face and head. They should try to block the shot as far in front of the goal as possible and, if blocked, attempt to control the ball and execute either of three options to return the ball into play.

Position in front of attacker.

Extend arms up to block.

Functional Profiles and General Modifications

As in wheelchair basketball, not all students will be able to execute the skills described for this sport. The athlete classification systems employed by the sporting organizations that play indoor wheelchair soccer use a more functional description of the athletes allowed to play.

Student Functional Profiles

Table 4.2 is a modification of the suggested classifications for students with disabilities designated to play. Read the table to see if you have students that might fit these profiles. A student that has multiple disabilities, such as quadriplegic athetoid cerebral palsy and visual impairment, might fit the low functional skill level.

Table 4.2	Student Functional Profiles for Indoor Wheelchair Soccer
Functional skill level	**Student profile**
Low	Severe disabilities in all four extremities; uses an electric or power wheelchair
Low to moderate	Severe to moderate disabilities in three of the four extremities; can use a manual wheelchair for short distances
Moderate	Minimal paraplegic (two lower) or hemiplegic (one side) disabilities; uses a manual wheelchair and can push the wheelchair at a moderate to high level
High	No neurological or physical disability in the upper extremity or trunk; has some severe disability in at least one lower extremity

General Modifications

In table 4.3, you will read how you might apply general modifications to the five skills necessary to play indoor wheelchair soccer. Notice that these modifications are suggested according to the student functional profiles. Again, it will be up to you to decide which skills and what modifications are appropriate for your situation.

Table 4.3	General Modifications for Indoor Wheelchair Soccer	
Skill level	**Skill**	**Activity modifications**
Low	Passing	Use a smaller ball.
	Shooting	Strike the ball into the goal area or push it into the goal with the wheelchair.
		Throw ball or beanbag into a wider goal area.
	Dribbling	Push a ball larger than 10 in. Attach a cardboard bumper to the front of the wheelchair.
	Throw-in	Knock a ball off a table or traffic cone into the court. Push the ball into the court with the wheelchair.
	Blocking	Block a rolled ball.

(continued)

Table 4.3	*(Continued)*	
Skill level	**Skill**	**Activity modifications**
Low to moderate	Passing	Shoot from a designated area to minimize wheelchair pushing.
	Shooting	Keep a three-foot space between defensive players at all times.
	Dribbling	Use two-handed dribble and have 5 sec instead of 3 sec to control the ball.
	Throw-in	More time to throw in
		Classmate assists, for example, stabilizes the ball in position before a throw-in.
	Blocking	Practice blocking each swing of a ball tethered from a basketball goal.
Moderate to high	All skills	No modifications: Used with highest-functioning students.

Game Progressions

The games listed in the remainder of this chapter are presented in progression from individual, to small group, to teamwork. Students should start out in activities with an individual focus and then move on to small group and teamwork activities as they improve, or according to their functional abilities. Keep in mind that inclusion means trying to address the three domains of physical education: psychomotor, cognitive, and affective.

Games-by-Skill-Level Index: Low-Functioning Students

The skill-level index in table 4.4 presents the games according to the functional level of your students. This index is for low- or severe-functioning students and is followed by game descriptions for this population. The index for higher-functioning students and game descriptions for that population follow the game description section for the lower-functioning population. Find the skill you want to address and cross-reference it with the level of activity you desire (individual, small group, or teamwork).

Table 4.4	**Games-by-Skill-Level Index for Low-Functioning Students—Indoor Wheelchair Soccer**		
Skills	**Individual activity**	**Small group activity**	**Teamwork**
Passing	Pass It On I	Pass It On II	Capture It
Shooting	Charge!	Rebound	Score It
Dribbling	Bump and Go I	Bump and Go II	Beat the Clock
Throw-in	Knock It Off I	Knock It Off II	Knock It Off III
Blocking	Keep It Out I	Keep It Out II	Keep It Out III

Game Descriptions

Each game description in this section includes game level, formation, equipment, description, extension, and inclusion suggestions. You will notice again that some games are presented in sequence, such as Knock It Off I, Knock It Off II, and Knock It Off III. You are not bound by the sequence, as this text is offered with the flexibility of your teaching situation in mind.

Skill Passing

◆ Pass It On I

Game Level: Individual

Formation: Individual with peer assistant as needed

Equipment: Beanbag, small ball, Wiffle ball, or Nerf ball

Description: The student attempts to hold a beanbag or small ball in their lap as long as possible in a stationary position.

Extension: Once the student can control the object, they can move across the gym carrying the object to a teammate.

Inclusion Suggestion: The student can demonstrate to the class their ability to accomplish the activity.

◆ Pass It On II

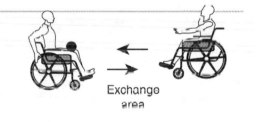

Exchange
area

Game Level: Small group

Formation: A continuation of Pass It On I, in which students on opposite sides of the free-throw lane face each other

Equipment: Beanbag, small ball, Wiffle ball, Nerf ball, beach ball

Description: One student has an object to control, such as a beanbag or beach ball. On a signal they move across the lane to their partner, where they exchange the object.

Extension: Vary the activity by increasing the distance, size, and weight of the object or by placing a time limit on the performance.

Inclusion Suggestions: Students with and without disabilities can participate. The student with a disability can call out the other student's name as they pass the object. The student with a disability may also suggest one modification for how the object should be carried.

◆ **Capture It**

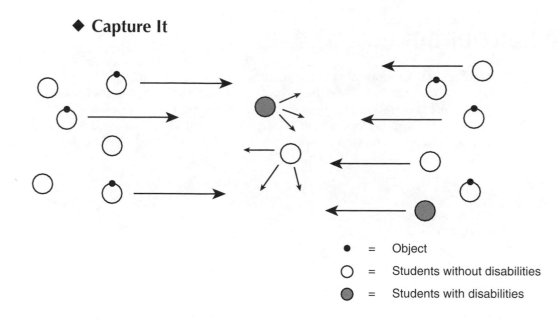

● = Object

○ = Students without disabilities

⬤ = Students with disabilities

Game Level: Teamwork

Formation: The class is in two teams, half at one end of the gym and the other half at the opposite end.

Equipment: 10-inch playground ball, beanbag, small ball, Wiffle ball, Nerf ball, or beach ball

Description: Three students from each team have an object to pass, such as a small ball, a beanbag, or a 10-inch playground ball. Two students, one with disabilities and one without disabilities, are in the middle of the gym. On a signal, both teams try to exchange places to the opposite end of the gym while passing the objects. As the teams exchange places, the students in the middle try to capture the balls or objects away from either team. If an object is captured, the student last in control exchanges places with the student in the middle for the next exchange.

Extension: The student with a disability can only play the middle position two consecutive times.

Inclusion Suggestion: The student with a disability can verbalize or in some way suggest one modification of how the groups should be allowed to move (forward, backward, two pushes, stop and go, and so on).

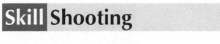
Skill Shooting

◆ Charge!

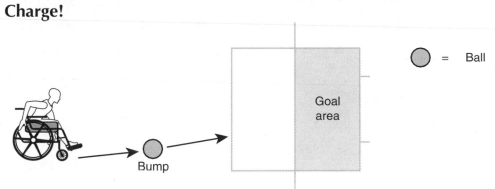

Game Level: Individual

Formation: Individual with peer assistant as needed

Equipment: 10-inch playground ball, beach ball, or basketball

Description: A larger sized ball is on the floor in front of the power wheelchair approximately six feet in front of the goal. The student with a disability takes a moving start at the ball and bumps or pushes it into the goal area.

Extension: Vary the distance and angle of the shot on goal.

Inclusion Suggestion: The student can demonstrate to the class their ability to accomplish the activity.

◆ Rebound

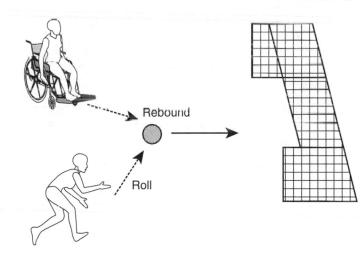

Game Level: Small group

Formation: Two students, one with and one without disabilities, in a triangle position, using the goal area as the third point of the triangle

Equipment: 10-inch playground ball, beach ball, or basketball

Description: The student without a disability rolls a ball on the floor in front of the goal area so that the student using the wheelchair can attack the ball and rebound it into the goal.

Extension: Change the angle of roll, position of roll, and speed of roll.

Inclusion Suggestion: The student with a disability can decide where to reposition the student rolling the ball.

◆ Score It

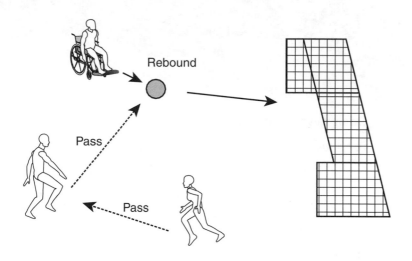

Game Level: Teamwork

Formation: Same starting positions as in the game Rebound, with the following change: use three students to pass the ball before attempting to shoot it into the goal.

Equipment: 10-inch playground ball, beach ball, or basketball

Description: Two passes must occur before the team can score, and the passes can come from any student. However, all three students must be involved with the play before scoring.

Extension: Increase the difficulty of this game by placing a defender in the group. As the teamwork gets better, rotate the defender with the player that scores the goal and restart the game.

Inclusion Suggestions: The student with a disability can decide who will initiate the first pass or communicate two additional skills to add to this game.

Skill Dribbling

◆ Bump and Go I

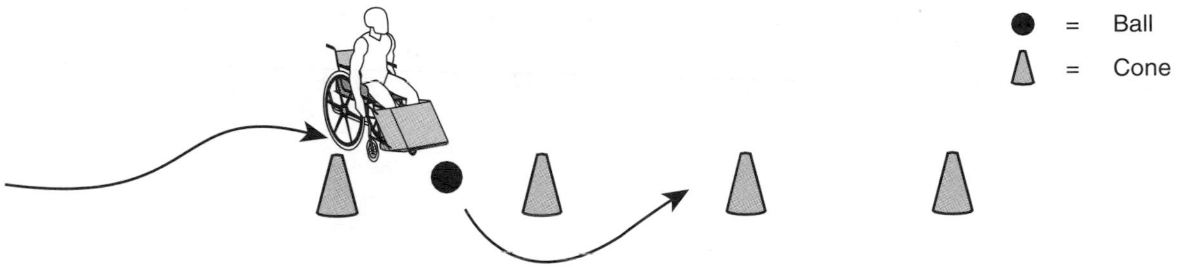

● = Ball

△ = Cone

Game Level: Individual

Formation: A series of traffic cones in a line formation with about six feet between each cone. A ball larger than 10 inches in diameter is in front of the power wheelchair.

Equipment: 10-inch or larger playground ball, traffic cones, sheet of cardboard, bands for attaching cardboard to wheelchair

Description: The student maneuvers through the traffic cones while controlling the ball. A large piece of cardboard attached to the front of the wheelchair with bungee cords can help the student control the ball.

Extension: Vary the distance between the cones.

Inclusion Suggestion: The student with a disability is in charge of creating a new pattern for moving through the cones (for example, every other cone).

◆ Bump and Go II

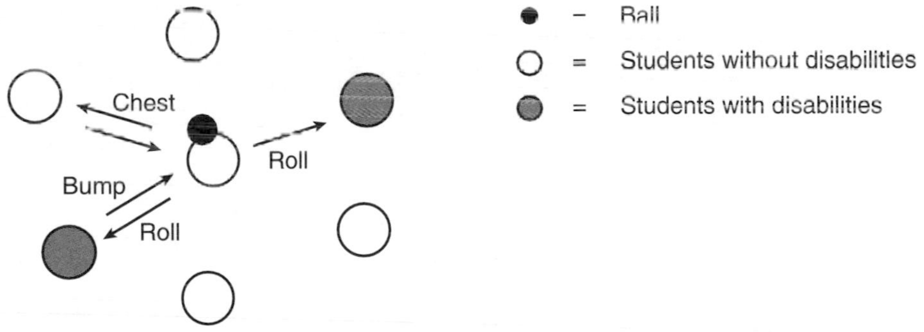

● – Ball

○ = Students without disabilities

◉ = Students with disabilities

Game Level: Small group

Formation: Students with and without disabilities in a circle formation with a student without a disability in the center holding a 10-inch playground ball

Equipment: 10-inch playground ball, beach ball, or Nerf volleyball

Description: On a signal the student in the center passes the ball around the circle using either a chest pass to students without disabilities or a rolled pass to those with disabilities. Students without disabilities catch the ball, perform three left, then three right-handed dribbles, and pass it back to the center. The student with a disability tries to bump the ball back to the center of the circle, using the front of their wheelchair.

Extension: Increase the size of the circle and the number of dribbles to be completed. Try completing the activity with two balls moving around at one time.

Inclusion Suggestion: The student with a disability can be in charge of creating a new pattern for moving the ball around the circle (for example, to every other person).

◆ Beat the Clock

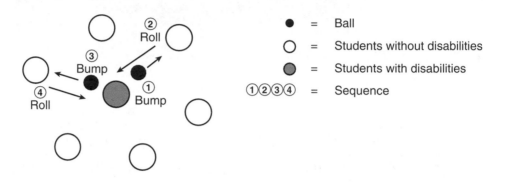

Game Level: Teamwork

Formation: Same formation as Bump and Go II, only this time a student with a disability is in the center of the circle

Equipment: 10-inch playground ball, beach ball, Nerf volleyball

Description: The ball starts in the center and the student bumps the ball out to the other students. The other students must pick up the ball and roll it back to the middle, where the student using the wheelchair bumps or dribbles the ball back out to the next student. The objective is to continue this ball movement around the circle.

Extension: Create several circles and have each group attempt to move the ball around in the shortest amount of time.

Inclusion Suggestion: The student with a disability can be in charge of choosing the next center player.

Skill Throw-In

◆ Knock It Off I

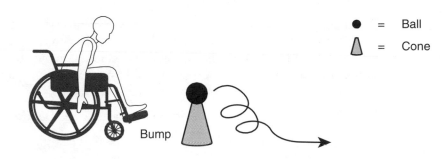

● = Ball
△ = Cone

Game Level: Individual

Formation: A large ball balanced on top of a tall traffic cone or table

Equipment: 10-inch or larger playground ball, tall traffic cones, folding table, bench, plastic floor hockey stick

Description: The student in a wheelchair approaches the ball rapidly. The student may use any part of their wheelchair or body to knock the ball off the cone or table, making sure to avoid contact with the cone or table. The objective is to put the ball into play.

Extension: The student may use an object to strike the ball from the cone or tabletop.

Inclusion Suggestion: The student should practice this activity with wheelchair control in mind and be able to demonstrate to their classmates the successful completion of this activity. The student should be able to judge the amount of wheelchair speed needed to knock the ball off the cone and safely put the ball into play.

◆ Knock It Off II

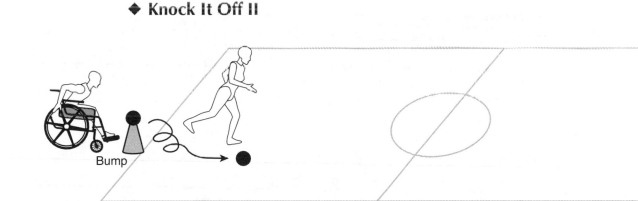

Game Level: Small group

Formation: Same starting formation as in Knock It Off I

Equipment: 10-inch or larger playground ball, tall traffic cones, folding table, bench, plastic floor hockey stick

Description: This time the student placing the ball into play (throwing in) must anticipate their approach so that they knock the ball into play as a teammate is passing in front of the cone. Students without disabilities are positioned in the court area, and on the signal move to the throw-in as if to receive the ball. The student throwing the ball into play must do so as their teammate is in position to receive the ball.

Extension: The student may use an object to strike the ball from the cone or tabletop.

Inclusion Suggestion: The student with a disability can give the starting signal for their teammate to move into position to accept the throw-in.

◆ Knock It Off III

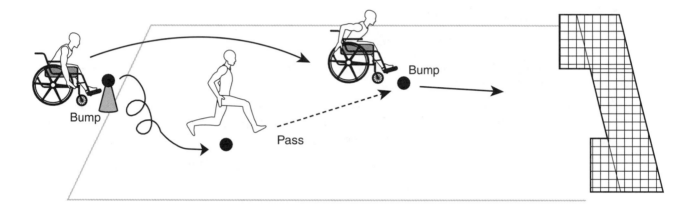

Game Level: Teamwork

Formation: Same starting formation as in Knock It Off II

Equipment: 10-inch or larger playground ball

Description: In this game, the students are closer to the goal. The student with a disability can throw the ball in (see Knock It Off I), and a student without a disability should receive the ball in the court area (see Knock It Off II). As the student in the court area receives the ball, the student with a disability moves on court and takes a pass from a teammate. They then attempt to bump the ball into the goal (see Bump and Go II).

Extension: Place a defender in the court to attempt a steal of the throw-in.

Inclusion Suggestion: The student with a disability can decide how the players should rotate positions for each throw-in by communicating verbally, visually, or by demonstration.

Skill Blocking

◆ Keep It Out I

●	=	Ball
▲	=	Cone
℮℮→	=	Rolled ball

Game Level: Individual

Formation: A student with a disability is between two traffic cones approximately 15 feet apart.

Equipment: 10-inch or larger playground ball, traffic cones

Description: A student without a disability rolls a ball at the student with a disability, attempting to roll the ball between the cones. The objective of the game is for the student with a disability to position their wheelchair to block the ball from passing between the cones.

Extension: Vary the distance rolled, the tempo of the roll, and the angle of the roll to help improve the defensive blocking.

Inclusion Suggestion: The student with a disability can determine the distance between cones to either increase or decrease the difficulty of the activity.

◆ Keep It Out II

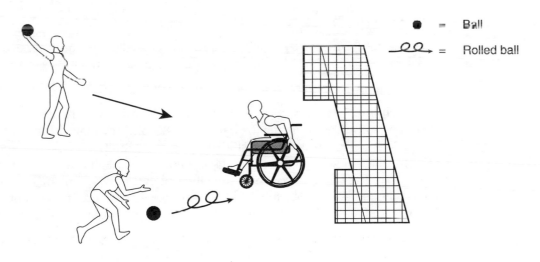

●	=	Ball
℮℮→	=	Rolled ball

Game Level: Small group

Formation: The student with a disability is in the position of goalkeeper in front of the goal or net.

Equipment: 10-inch or larger playground ball, traffic cones, gym mats as goals

Description: Two students without disabilities roll and/or bounce a ball toward the goal. As this occurs, the student with a disability attempts to block the ball from entering the goal or net.

Extensions: Vary the distance rolled, the tempo of the roll, and the angle of the roll to help improve the defensive blocking. Start with one ball at a time, then progress to two balls thrown alternately toward the net at a faster pace.

Inclusion Suggestions: The student with a disability can determine the distance of the throw at the goal or net, or the rotation of players during the activity.

◆ Keep It Out III

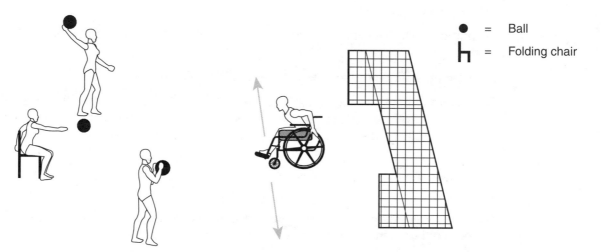

● = Ball

h = Folding chair

Game Level: Teamwork

Formation: One student with a disability as goalkeeper and three or four students without disabilities 15 feet in front of the net, each with a ball

Equipment: 10-inch or larger playground ball, traffic cones, gym mats as goals

Description: Using a random order, the students without disabilities attempt shots on the goal by rolling or bouncing the ball into the goal. They may not throw the ball into the net. The objective is for the student with a disability to position and/or reposition themselves after each shot to block the goal attempt. The teacher should control the tempo of the shots on goal but allow the students to shoot in any random order. Once each student has taken a turn, students can rotate positions. The student with a disability can bump the ball into the net as their shot attempt from a pass by their teammate.

Extension: Students without disabilities may be positioned on their knees in goalkeeper position and can only block using their nondominant arm.

Inclusion Suggestions: The student with a disability can determine the rotation of shots by players during the activity. The student can also report shots blocked versus goals scored.

Games-by-Skill-Level Index: Moderate- to High-Functioning Students

Table 4.5 is designed to address those students with moderate to high function. The progression of activity suggestions remains the same: individual, to small group, to teamwork.

Table 4.5	Games-by-Skill-Level Index for Moderate- to High-Functioning Students—Indoor Wheelchair Soccer		
Skills	**Individual activity**	**Small group activity**	**Teamwork**
Passing	Target Toss	Partner Pass	Call It Out
Shooting	Feed Me	Feed and Go	Feed and Go Plus I
Dribbling	Stationary	On the Move I	One the Move II
Throw-in	Reach Back	Pick a Spot	Pick a Spot with "D"
Blocking	Pin Block	Feed and Go	Feed and Go Plus I

Game Descriptions

The 15 games suggested in this next section are designed to help you teach your moderate- to high-functioning students with disabilities in your classes. Modify any or all of these games to meet your needs. Keep in mind the approach to inclusion mentioned throughout this book.

Skill Passing (Two-Handed, Bounce, and Baseball Pass)

◆ Target Toss

Game Level: Individual

Formation: Individual with peer assistant as needed

Equipment: 10-inch playground ball, targets for wall, cones for distance markers

Description: After reviewing each of the key points for executing the two-handed and baseball passes, the student with a disability passes the ball into a target (e.g., a two-foot-diameter circle) from a distance of six to eight feet.

Extensions: Higher-skilled students can pass with the nondominant hand. Students without disabilities can assist retrieving and providing appropriate feedback.

Inclusion Suggestions: The student can demonstrate to the class their ability to accomplish the activity and determine three new distances for the target. The student can also determine two additional skills to be added to this activity.

◆ Partner Pass

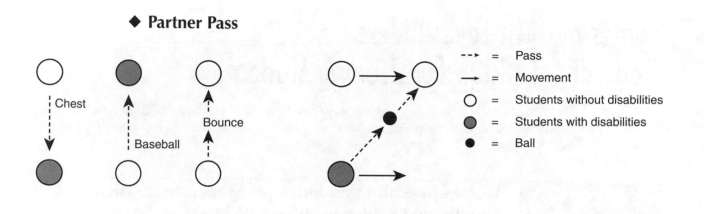

Game Level: Small group

Formation: Students with and without disabilities are in two parallel lines facing each other about 15 feet apart.

Equipment: 10-inch playground ball

Description: Using the two-handed pass or baseball pass, students try to pass to their partner from a stationary position. Score one point for passes that are complete and subtract two points for each errant pass, or set up any type of scoring activity that would work for you.

Extension: Once they are successful with stationary passing, the partners move across the gym floor using either of the two passes.

Inclusion Suggestion: The student with a disability can be in charge of determining the type of pass to be used for each trip across the gym and reporting the score at the end of each trip.

◆ Call It Out

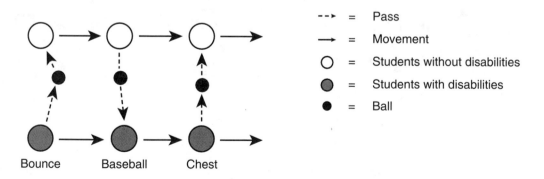

Game Level: Teamwork

Formation: Students are in parallel line formation opposite a partner. This is a dynamic formation with students moving forward in pairs as they pass the ball. Students with and without disabilities should be paired up.

Equipment: 10-inch playground ball

Description: Each set of partners has a 10-inch playground ball and on the signal must move forward across the floor, passing the ball as they move. Partners must stay about 15 to 20 feet apart and emphasize keeping the ball ahead of their partner. The teacher changes the type of pass every two or three trips down the floor by calling out a new pass (for example, two-handed pass, bounce pass, baseball pass). The objective is to complete one trip without a miss using each of the passes.

Extension: For students with varying degrees of manual propulsion, change the type of ball used to pass and/or the distance passed.

Inclusion Suggestion: The student with a disability can call out the pass to be executed.

Skill Shooting

◆ Feed Me

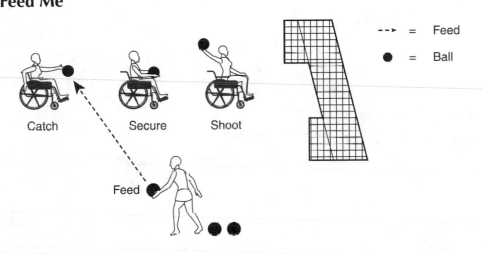

Game Level: Individual

Formation: One student without a disability is at the corner of the goal net with three 10-inch playground balls. The student with a disability is positioned about 13 to 15 feet in front of the net.

Equipment: 10-inch playground ball, goal or gym mats to simulate goal

Description: The purpose of this activity is for the student with moderate to high functional ability to practice catching, securing, and shooting the ball into the goal area. On a signal, the student using the wheelchair moves forward toward the goal as the student with the playground balls "feeds" the student in the wheelchair with a pass. The student using the wheelchair must catch, secure, and shoot the ball into the net using the same movements as taught during the passing skills (that is, either a two-handed push shot or a baseball throw). As soon as the shot is taken, the student in the wheelchair recovers and repositions at the starting point and the activity is continued.

Extension: Vary the distance and angle of shot on goal.

Inclusion Suggestion: The student with a disability may suggest one new skill to the activity.

◆ Feed and Go

Game Level: Small group

Formation: Same formation as Feed Me; however, now the activity is started at the center circle area.

Equipment: 10-inch playground ball, goal or gym mats to simulate goal

Description: The student using the wheelchair catches the ball (feed) and secures the ball for a count of three seconds as they are moving toward the net (go). As they move closer to the net, they shoot using either a two-handed shot or a baseball type throw.

Extension: Rotate the student with a disability to the feeder position.

Inclusion Suggestion: The student with a disability can report to the teacher where the shot on goal went (for instance, high and in the corner or low and in the middle).

◆ Feed and Go Plus 1

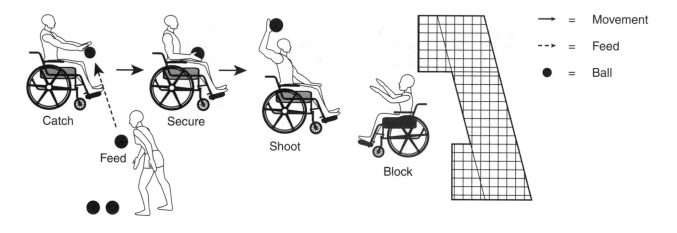

Catch Feed Secure Shoot Block

→ = Movement
--► = Feed
● = Ball

Game Level: Teamwork

Formation: Same formation as Feed and Go, except a third person is added to the activity (plus 1) as a defender

Equipment: 10-inch playground ball, goal or gym mats to simulate goal

Description: The defender is positioned as the goalkeeper and attempts to block the shot taken.

Extensions: Rotate the students through each of the positions (for example, the student feeding moves to the shooter position, the shooter moves to goalkeeper, and the goalkeeper moves to feeder). Students with and without disabilities can be placed at any of the positions. Adjust the distance of shot, speed of movement, and tempo of pass according to students' abilities.

Inclusion Suggestions: The student with a disability can determine the order of rotation or establish one new version of the activity (for example, adding a second defender).

Skill Dribbling (Push Dribble Only)

◆ Stationary

Game Level: Individual

Formation: This is the same activity described for wheelchair basketball using the 10-inch playground ball. The purpose of this activity is to allow the student with moderate or high functional ability to practice dribbling the ball in a stationary position.

Equipment: 10-inch playground ball, folding chairs, benches

Description: Students with less functional ability could start with a two-handed bounce and catch while leaning to the side of the wheelchair.

Extensions: Students having difficulty controlling a regulation 10-inch playground ball might try one slightly deflated (less than two psi). Students without disabilities could be included in this activity by participating from folding chairs or benches.

Inclusion Suggestion: The student with a disability can decide a set number of successful dribbles to accomplish before changing hands (for example, 10 with the right hand, then 10 with the left).

◆ On the Move I

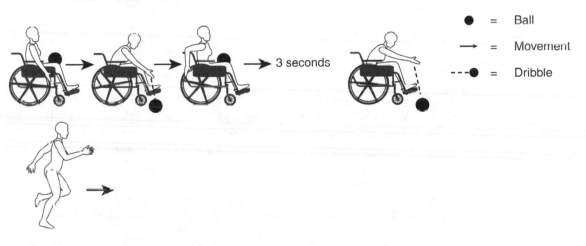

● = Ball

→ = Movement

---● = Dribble

3 seconds

Game Level: Small group

Formation: The student with a disability is partnered with a student without a disability in a side-by-side formation facing the same direction and ready to move across the gym floor.

Equipment: 10-inch playground ball, folding chairs, benches

Description: The student with a disability pushes forward in their wheelchair while carrying the ball in their lap. Once they are moving, they must dribble using one hand while controlling their wheelchair. They may return the ball to their lap after traveling 15 feet but must return to dribbling within the three-second time limit. The student without a disability walks next to the wheelchair to help with errant dribbling. The student continues the activity across the gymnasium floor. On the return trip, the student without a disability performs the dribble using proper techniques, and the student with a disability serves as the assistant recovering errant dribbles.

Extension: Increase the difficulty of this activity by placing traffic cones in a line about six to eight feet apart, and instruct the students to dribble in a weave pattern in and out among the cones.

Inclusion Suggestion: The student without a disability performs the dribble in both directions while the student with a disability critiques their movement. At the end of both trips across the gym, the student with a disability shares which aspects look correct and which movements need work. The two students then reverse rolls and repeat the activity.

◆ On the Move II

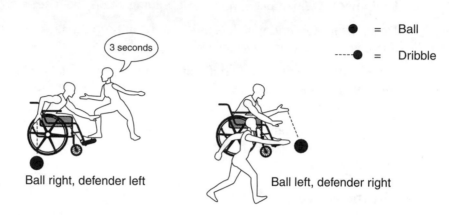

3 seconds

Ball right, defender left

Ball left, defender right

● = Ball

----● = Dribble

Game Level: Teamwork

Formation: Same position as On the Move I

Equipment: 10-inch playground ball, folding chairs, benches

Description: With this activity the student without a disability challenges the dribble by representing a defender and changing positions next to the wheelchair. With each attempt at dribbling, the student with a disability must keep the ball on the opposite side of the wheelchair away from the defender; that is, as the student with a disability dribbles the ball on the right side, the defender should be on the left; and as the defender switches to the other side, so should the dribbler. The student without a disability counts out loud for three seconds each time the student using the wheelchair places the ball in their lap as they change positions.

Extension: Try this activity in a stationary formation before moving across the gym floor.

Inclusion Suggestions: The student with a disability can decide who starts first with the ball. The same student can count successful switches from side to side and report the count to the teacher.

Skill Throw-In

◆ Reach Back

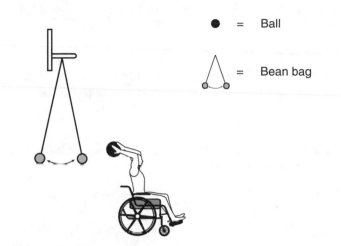

● = Ball

△ = Bean bag

Game Level: Individual

Formation: The student with a disability is under a basketball goal holding a 10-inch playground ball in both hands. A beanbag is suspended from the basketball goal so that it hangs about eight inches above and behind the student's head.

Equipment: 10-inch playground ball, basketball goal and backboard, rope, beanbag

Description: The student raises the ball into the throw-in position, using both arms if possible, and tries to strike the beanbag with the ball while bringing it behind their head to perform the throw-in facing the court. The student must reach back as much as possible to ensure a legal throw-in.

Extension: Adjust the length of the rope to increase or decrease the student's reach.

Inclusion Suggestion: The student with a disability can tell the teacher how much to increase or decrease the length of the rope.

◆ Pick a Spot

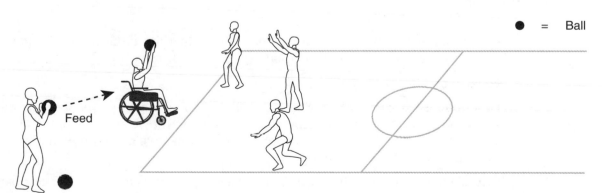

● = Ball

Feed

Game Level: Small group

Formation: A student with a disability is in the throw-in position on the sideline of the court facing the playing area, and a student without a disability is next to them serving as a feeder for this activity. Three or four students with or without disabilities in a semicircular formation are about 15 to 20 feet away in the playing area facing the throw-in.

Equipment: 10-inch playground ball

Description: On a signal the student in-bounds the ball using the throw-in skill to any of the players in the court. As soon as one ball is thrown in, another one is ready for the student to repeat the throw-in. This activity continues until all students in the playing area have received a ball.

Extension: Adjust the distance to the student on the court, either increasing or decreasing the distance for the throw-in.

Inclusion Suggestion: The student with a disability can call out the other student's name before throwing in the ball. If the student is nonverbal, they can use another form of communication, such as pointing or nodding in the direction of the throw-in.

◆ Pick a Spot With "D"

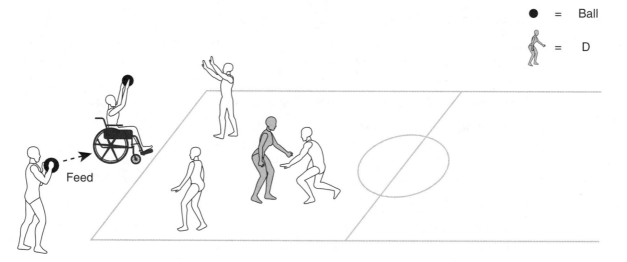

● = Ball

= D

Game Level: Teamwork

Formation: Same position as Pick a Spot, except that the distance of the throw-in is increased and a defender (D) is added

Equipment: 10-inch playground ball

Description: A student with or without disabilities is between the player performing the throw-in and the players trying to receive the throw-in. The objective is for the student to complete as many throw-ins as possible without the "D" intercepting the ball. Students rotate positions after one minute.

Extension: The student without a disability acting as a defender may use a scooter board.

Inclusion Suggestions: The student with a disability can call out the other student's name before throwing in the ball. If the student is nonverbal, they may use another form of communication, such as pointing or nodding in the direction of the throw-in. The student can also report the number of successful throw-ins during the activity.

Skill Blocking

◆ Pin Block

Game Level: Individual

Formation: Three or four plastic bowling pins (or other like objects) arranged on a bench or table to be used as targets. A student with a disability is in front of the pins to serve as a defender.

Equipment: 10-inch playground ball, plastic bowling pins, bench

Description: A student with or without disabilities throws the playground ball at the pins attempting to knock them off one by one. The student defending must position to block the shot attempt and not allow the pins to fall. After each shot, the student shooting must allow the defender to reposition before the next shot. Shooting distance must be greater than 19 feet.

Extension: Change the shooting distance, size of the ball, or texture of the ball (Nerf ball). Students without disabilities can throw with their nondominant hand and/or play the defender position from their knees or sitting on gym scooters.

Inclusion Suggestion: The student with a disability can choose the first defender.

◆ Feed and Go

Game Level: Small group

Formation: Same activity as described for Feed and Go in the skill of shooting, except that the emphasis is on blocking rather than shooting

Equipment: Ten-inch playground ball, goal or gym mats to simulate goal

Description: The student using the wheelchair catches the ball (feed) and secures the ball for a count of three seconds as they move toward the net (go). As they move closer to the net, they shoot using either a two-handed shot or a baseball pass.

Extension: Rotate the student with a disability to the feeder position.

Inclusion Suggestion: The student with a disability can report to the teacher how many shots were blocked.

◆ Feed and Go Plus 1

Game Level: Teamwork

Formation: Same formation as in Feed and Go, except a third person is added to the activity (plus 1) as a defender and the emphasis is on blocking

Equipment: 10-inch playground ball, goal or gym mats to simulate goal

Description: The defender is positioned as the goalkeeper and attempts to block the shot taken.

Extensions: You can rotate the students through each of the positions. For example, the student feeding can move to the shooter position, the shooter can move to the goalkeeper position, and the goalkeeper can move to the feeder position. Students with and without disabilities can be placed at any of the positions. Adjust the distance of the shot, the speed of the movement, and the tempo of the pass according to your students' functional skill levels.

Inclusion Suggestions: The student with a disability can determine the order of rotation. The student may also establish one new version of the activity (for instance, add a second defender).

PART III

NET GAMES

Chapter 5 Sitting Volleyball

Chapter 6 Wheelchair Tennis

chapter

5

Sitting Volleyball

Sitting volleyball was established in the Netherlands in the mid-1950s by the Dutch Sports Committee. The sport was created by combining traditional volleyball with a German game called sitzball. Since its introduction, sitting volleyball, which includes individuals with and without disabilities, has grown to be one of the Netherlands' largest competitive sports.

The International Sports Organization for the Disabled (ISOD), which is a Paralympic organization, adopted sitting volleyball in the late 1970s. As of this writing, sitting volleyball has been in every Paralympic competition since 1980. Seven teams participated in the first year of Paralympic competition, although the United States did not compete until 1984. The inclusion of sitting volleyball has spread to other international competitions, including the World and European Championships for athletes with disabilities.

In the 1996 Atlanta Paralympics, 12 countries were entered in the sitting volleyball competition. The gold medal was won that year by the Islamic Republic of Iran. A strong showing from the European countries was very evident, as second through sixth place were won by Norway, Finland, the Netherlands, Germany, and Hungary, respectively. The United States' showing in Atlanta and then in Sydney indicates a stronger need to develop this sport in our country, as we finished eleventh and twelfth. In Europe sitting volleyball is the fastest growing sport for inclusion of individuals with and without disabilities. Try integrating this sport in your physical education curriculum and help further its development and growth in this country.

Description of the Sport

The sport of sitting volleyball has many similarities to regulation volleyball. In fact, the four skills mentioned in this chapter are exactly the same as those used in regulation volleyball: pass (overhead and forearm, to include the set), attack-hit, block, and serve. The objective of the game is to send the ball over the net so that it is not returned by the opponent—in other words, to ground the ball on the opponents' court.

The ball is put into play with a serve, and each team is allowed three hits to return it to the opponents' court. A block of a hit ball is not counted as one of the three hits. Once the ball has been put into play after the serve, each team attempts to return the ball to the opponents' court, or "rally the ball," by using passing skills.

Rally scoring is used to score in sitting volleyball. Rally scoring means points can be awarded to the offense or defense on a ball not returned to the opponents' court. When the nonserving team wins a rally, it is awarded a point and the right to serve. Former rules for scoring allowed only the serving team to score points by winning a rally. Each time the receiving team wins a rally and a serve, they must rotate player positions one place in a clockwise direction.

Field of Play

The game is played on a court measuring 40 feet by 20 feet. A regulation court for standing volleyball is 60 feet in length by 30 feet in width. The attack line in sitting volleyball is shorter, measuring six feet six inches back and perpendicular to the center line, rather than 23 feet as in standing volleyball.

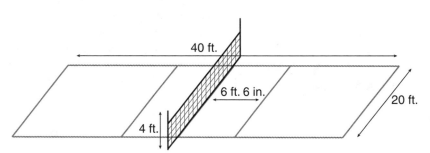

Sitting volleyball court.

Players

Any person with a permanent lower-body impairment is eligible to play; however, all players must play from a seated position on the floor. Individuals with amputations, *les autres* conditions, cerebral palsy, or spinal cord injuries, and who are considered paraplegic, are eligible to play. *Les autres* ("the other") conditions may include polio, muscular dystrophy, and/or multiple sclerosis. In official competition, athletes must be classified using a sports classification system, and all athletes must meet a "minimal disability" criterion. Minimal disability means the athlete must have a disability severe enough to prevent them from playing in a regulation volleyball game for individuals without disabilities.

Equipment

The height of the net is four feet for men and three feet six inches for women. The ball is usually a lighter color (white) and approximately 65 to 67 centimeters in circumference. The ball should be inflated to the proper pressure as suggested by the manufacturer. Players in an official sitting volleyball match may wear long pants, and they must sit directly on the floor. Players are not allowed to sit on thick padding while on the court of play. You can, of course, modify this rule in your physical education class, as you may want your students to sit on a wrestling mat for comfort. You can use a lighter ball and a lower net for students with more severe disabilities. As always, make any modifications necessary for your teaching situation.

Starting the Game

The game is started by first deciding which team will serve, which is accomplished by a coin toss. The team winning the toss chooses either to serve first or defend a preferred court. Games are played to 25 points using rally scoring. Remember that with rally scoring it is possible for the receiving team to score points despite not having served. An official team consists of 12 players, but only 6 are on the court at one time. All player positions are determined by the position of the buttocks on the floor and not the position of legs or arms. For example, it is possible for a player who does not have use of their legs to be seated in the court area but have their legs positioned outside the court.

Game Objective

The objective of the game is the same as in regulation or standing volleyball, and that is to rally the ball in such a manner as to ground it on the opponents' court. Grounding the ball in the opponents' court may come from a serve, a well-placed pass, or an attack-hit. Teams are allowed three touches to rally the ball to the opponents' court in an attempt to ground the ball.

Team formations are similar to those in standing volleyball. The two rows of three players are considered front-row and back-row players. Blocking the serve by front-row players is allowed when the ball is in the front area of the court and positioned higher than the top of the net. A back-row player in sitting volleyball may carry out an attack-hit from any ball height, provided that the player's buttocks do not touch or cross over the front attack line.

Offensively, teams should work on passing the ball as setups for attack-hits. As players develop their skills, they need to consider passing the ball with appropriate height and speed to a teammate. A high pass is characterized by a high, arching slower-paced pass to a teammate, either from the back to the front row or from side to side. A moderate pass is one in which the pass is more deliberate and direct, with less arch and more speed. The quickest pass is one that is flat and fast-paced to be used in quick setting for attack-hits. All three of these passes are subject to your students' ability levels and should be considered only if you feel they are appropriate.

Players move on the court from a seated position by using their hands and arms to momentarily lift the buttocks from the floor and slide to a new position. No standing is allowed to move to a new position. Players must have the ability to move in all directions. Generally, players travel three to six feet to rally a ball with teammates. Once in position to rally a ball, players should have adequate trunk stability and balance to hold themselves in position for the play. Players may use their nonstriking arms as support for balance during an attack-hit or while serving a ball.

Defensively, players attempting to block a ball at the net should have substantial sitting balance and trunk stability. A block is performed by extending both arms straight up, palms facing the net and less than two inches apart, and leaning slightly forward with the intent of sending the ball directly back to the opponents' court. One-arm blocks are possible; however, players must be able to brace themselves with one arm to the floor, reach up as high as possible, and block the ball without losing balance. Generally speaking, one-arm blocks are not as effective at the net but can be successful further back on the court.

Remember, you can change the rules, equipment, player formations, or court size and can conduct the game according to your needs. Try to get your students to perform this sequence of skills in an attempt to ground the ball in the opponents' court: pass, set, and attack-hit. These three basic skills will help them conduct successful rallies in sitting volleyball.

Game Length

The World Organization of Volleyball for the Disabled (WOVD) determined for the 2000 Paralympic Games that the sitting volleyball competition would use rally scoring with games to 25 points. Teams had to win by at least two points. All matches included five games, with the winner of three games declared the overall winner. Tie-breaker games had to be played to 15 points, and teams had to win by two points.

General Rules/Penalties

As previously mentioned, many of the rules for sitting volleyball are similar to those for regulation volleyball. Following are the rules that are specific to sitting volleyball.

Rules Specific to Sitting Volleyball

The court size is smaller (40 by 20 feet); attack lines are closer to the net (six feet, six inches); and the net height, length, and width are all reduced for the sport of sitting volleyball. Player positions are determined by where the player is seated, not by the position of arms or legs. This rule allows the player's impaired limbs to touch out-of-bound lines without penalty. Players are allowed to wear long pants during play; however, special padded material is not allowed underneath the player.

All players in an official sitting volleyball contest must be considered disabled, but two players on the roster are allowed to be evaluated as "minimally disabled." Only one player classified as minimally disabled is allowed on the court during an actual game. An example of minimally disabled would be a person who has a lower-body impairment but ambulates unassisted (such as a person with a below-knee amputation). Individuals with single-leg amputations are eligible to play both sitting and standing volleyball.

Player positions are determined by the contact point of the players' buttocks and the floor. Player positions in standing volleyball are determined by the contact point of the players' feet. During a serve, the player's buttocks must remain in the service area and cannot make contact with the court area. Again, a player's feet or legs may touch the opponents' court during play as long as there is no interference with play. If a player's feet or legs touch the opponents' court during play, the player must return them to their own court as soon as possible.

A special rule for front-row players concerning blocking service is different from the rules of standing volleyball. When defending a serve, front-row players in sitting volleyball are allowed to block the service of the opponent. Also, at the 2000 Paralympics it was ruled that balls touching the net during a serve be allowed for play and not considered an infraction, forcing a side-out.

During a rally, players are not allowed to stand up or take steps to reposition themselves on the court. Players must remain in contact with the court with any part of their body between their shoulders and hips or buttocks. A momentary lifting of the buttocks is allowed during play.

Summary of the Sport

Table 5.1 is an overview of sitting volleyball. Use this table as a quick reference to the game.

Table 5.1	Overview of Sitting Volleyball
Field of play	The court is 40 by 20 ft. Attack lines are drawn 6 ft 6 in. from the center line.
Players	Maximum allowed on court is six players. Only one can be classified as minimally disabled.
Equipment	The net is 21 ft long and 2 ft 6 in. wide and is 4 ft high for men and 3 ft 6 in. high for women. The ball is a regulation volleyball usually 65-67 cm in circumference.
Legal start and scoring	The game is started with a serve. The player must be in the service area and in contact with the floor. Balls touching the net on a serve are legal. Rally scoring is used to score games to 25 points. In regulation matches, the winning team must win three of five games.
Ball movement	The ball is moved by either a pass (to include set), attack-hit, or serve. Only three touches are allowed on one team to move the ball across the net to the opponents' court during a rally.
Player positions	There are two rows with three players in each row. All player positions are established by the contact of the player's buttocks and the court. There are two front row attackers, one setter, and three back-row players.
Player movement during play	Touching feet/legs to the opponents' court is permitted at any time during the play, provided that the player does not interfere with an opposing player. Touching the opponents' court with a hand is permitted; again, the player should avoid interference during the game. Defenders may attempt to block the serve.

Skills to Be Taught

Four skills can be taught in your physical education class for sitting volleyball: the pass, the attack-hit, the block, and the serve. Notice that within the skill of passing there are two variations, overhead and forearm. Most teachers refer to these two passes as "set" and "bump," which is what they will be called in this chapter.

Players must have the ability to move about the court independently. Each player's method of movement is specific to their disability and will not be discussed in this chapter. However, you should encourage the student to learn to move quickly and anticipate the position of the ball during a rally. If your students are not capable of moving quickly while seated on the floor, you can slow the flight of the ball by changing the type of ball used in the game. You might consider using a beach ball or "volley light" ball, which is a ball sized like a volleyball but made of lightweight rubberized material similar to a Nerf ball.

Whether you choose to play on a padded surface or not, there are benefits for the student with a disability to playing volleyball on the floor. The greatest benefit is that the game allows the student to get out of the wheelchair and experience independent movement. Another advantage is that everyone can play on the floor, students with and without disabilities together, which helps to create an environment of inclusion. It is up to you to decide where and how to play sitting volleyball. The following skills are taken from the competitive sport but can be modified for your teaching situation.

Passing

The two types of passes used in the game of sitting volleyball are the overhead pass and the forearm pass. Feel free to teach these skills according to your students' abilities.

• **Overhead Pass (or Set).** Positioned under the ball facing the net, the student holds the hands at or near the forehead with thumbs together. As the ball approaches, the student spreads the fingers and flexes the wrists; the thumbs and forefingers should form a triangle or "window" to see the ball. The student makes contact with the ball cleanly with the pads of fingers and thumbs while extending the elbows forcefully up and through the ball. As the ball departs from the hands, there should be minimal to no rotation or spin. The same mechanics are used for the set; however, the location of the pass is the key difference.

When using the overhead pass to set a volleyball, the student should direct the ball using either of the three passes mentioned earlier: high, moderate, or quick. Placement of the set is critical to the execution of an attack-hit. The student should attempt to set the ball high and close enough to the net to allow an attack player to execute the hit. Sets are generally 6 to 18 inches from the net. The height of the set will be determined by the type of tempo used.

Contact the ball with the pads of the fingers for an overhead pass.

Extend the elbows forcefully, minimizing ball rotation.

- **Forearm Pass.** This pass is used to pass a ball received at or below waist height. This is a two-handed pass and should be executed by having the ball strike the wrists, the lower arms, or the tops of the thumbs. The student clasps hands by holding the thumb of the right hand with the fingers of the left hand, palms slightly turned upward. Arms are extended, with a slight flexion at the elbows; shoulders are internally rotated. At contact with the ball, the student attempts to pass the ball up with gentle force, trying to absorb the ball's impact as much as possible.

In regulation volleyball, players are told to bend their knees and lift as the ball is passed. Since such a maneuver is not possible for students with disabilities, they must develop a touch for absorbing the force of the ball when contact is made. This pass is often used to move a ball from the back row to the front row in preparation to set and attack-hit.

Preparation for the forearm pass.

Position under the ball, clasped hands and elbows extended.

Absorb the force of the ball's impact.

Attack-Hit

The attack-hit has also been referred to as the "kill" shot in volleyball and sitting volleyball. The attack-hit is a downward, forceful strike at the ball designed to ground the ball immediately on the opponents' court. To execute the attack-hit, the student should be in position underneath a descending ball and slightly behind its drop path, while facing the net. As the ball descends, the student rotates the striking shoulder away from the net and positions the striking arm back and away from the body, with wrist cocked. Contact with the ball is made by rotating the striking arm and shoulder forward and striking the ball with a slightly open hand at or near the top of the ball. The emphasis at contact is to strike the ball with a strong force resulting in a downward trajectory of the ball into the opponents' court. Contact should be made at the highest point possible above the net. The contact point will vary according to the student's functional ability and skill development.

Position the body under the ball with the arm and wrist ready.

Rotate the striking shoulder away from the net and position the striking arm back.

Contact the ball with a slightly open hand in a downward direction.

Block

The block is a skill that can be executed individually or with a teammate. It is performed by positioning as close to the net as possible, being careful not to interfere with the opponents' play. Remember, a student's limbs are allowed to pass under the net and lie in the opponents' court provided there is no interference. However, the student is responsible for keeping control of these limbs during play.

- **Individual Block.** Using a stable, balanced sitting position, the student reaches up with both arms, elbows fully extended and close together, and with palms facing toward the net. The block is performed by deflecting the ball directly back to the opponents' court in a downward pattern. Timing is the key component of this skill. The student must be able to time the blocking move appropriately in order to make it an effective defensive maneuver.

- **Two-Person Block.** To execute a two-person block at the net, students should practice moving into correct court position prior to attempting the block. A two-person block is performed the same as an individual block; however, both teammates must make every effort to align shoulders and arms parallel to the net. Blocking can occur away from the net but is often executed with one arm extended upward in an attempt to deflect the ball to a teammate for a possible set and attack-hit combination.

Position close to the net ready for a block.

Reach up with both arms; keep hands together for a block.

Two-person block.

Serve

The serve is used to put the ball into play at the beginning of a game. The serve described here will be the overhand serve. Although you may want to start your students with an underhand serve, competitive serves are usually made with the overhand technique.

To execute the overhand serve (right-handed), have the student sit facing the net with a slight rotation of the striking shoulder away from the net. The student should hold the ball in the left hand slightly higher than eye level, with the elbow extended. The right arm is drawn back as the elbow is flexed and the wrist cocked in position to strike the ball (see passing skill). To serve the ball, the student raises the left arm slightly above the forehead as the right arm is brought forward to strike the ball. Emphasize striking the ball from the support hand (left) with minimal vertical toss. Contact should be made

Hold the ball higher than eye level with the striking arm drawn back.

Raise the ball above the head and make contact with the heel of the hand and the fingers slightly open.

with the heel of the hand and cupped fingers at a point just above the head. It is important to emphasize follow-through on contact, as this will help direct the ball to the opponents' court. The motion is similar to the overhand throw in baseball.

Functional Profiles and General Modifications

Table 5.2 presents student profiles that might fit your teaching situation. Read the table to determine the functional level of your student(s), then consider the activity modifications listed in table 5.3.

Student Functional Profiles

These functional profiles are operationally defined as low, moderate, and high. In order to play sitting volleyball, players must have a fair degree of trunk stability and independent sitting balance; that is, they must be moderate to high functioning. Students considered low functioning are those who would not be able to hold a balanced seated position out of the wheelchair without some form of assistance. *All activities written for low-functioning students should be implemented with the student in the wheelchair* unless some form of assisted seating is provided (for example, support from a teacher or teacher's assistant).

Table 5.2	Student Functional Profiles for Sitting Volleyball
Functional skill level	**Student profile**
Low	Multiple impairments; unable to sit independently without trunk support; unable to move independently on the floor; might use an electric or power wheelchair.
Moderate	Able to sit independently for short durations; can sit independently by bracing with one arm to the floor; has moderate strength in upper body and can momentarily lift buttocks from floor while seated using two arms; able to move 3 ft independently on the floor.
High	Able to sustain a seated position on the floor without support; can lift buttocks from the floor and move 3-6 ft independently; is able to hold both arms overhead and maintain balance while in seated position without support; is able to lean backward to reach or strike a volleyball without losing balance when seated on the floor.

General Modifications

In table 5.3, you will read how you might apply general modifications for students with disabilities to the skills of sitting volleyball. Each modification is suggested according to the student functional profiles in table 5.2. You can decide how best to apply these general modifications to your unique student population.

Table 5.3	General Modifications for Sitting Volleyball	
Skill level	**Skill**	**Activity modifications**
Low	Passing	Roll a ball back and forth across the length of a table to a partner.
	Attack-hit	Strike a swinging lightweight ball to simulate an attack-hit.
	Block	From 2 ft in front of a tabletop, move the wheelchair to block a ball before it rolls off the table's edge. Balls come from any direction.
	Serve	Seated in front of a table with a ball tethered overhead, swing the ball forward over the table to the opposite end to simulate a serve.
Moderate	Passing	Seated on the floor, roll or toss a ball to another student.
	Attack-hit	Seated on the floor beside a tall traffic cone, balance a volleyball on the cone and strike the ball from the cone.
	Block	Seated on the floor beneath a ball tethered to a basketball rim, block the ball with two arms as it swings forward.
	Serve	Throw the ball from a serving position on the floor.
High	All skills	No modifications: Used with highest-functioning students.

Game Progressions

The games listed in the remainder of this chapter are presented in progression, from individual, to small group, to teamwork. Remember that students should start out with an individual activity and move into small group and teamwork situations as their skills improve. Higher-functioning students can of course begin with small group or teamwork activities as appropriate. These games are intended to help you include your students with disabilities in a volleyball unit. Keep in mind that students considered low functioning will have to perform these games from their wheelchairs. Also, remember that the inclusion suggestions are meant to help you place students with disabilities in more decision-making roles.

Games-by-Skill-Level Index: Low-Functioning Students

The index in table 5.4 will help you choose games for low-functioning students according to their needs. Find the skill you want to address in your class and cross reference it with the level of activity you desire (individual, small group, or teamwork). The index is followed by game descriptions that are written specifically for students who are lower functioning. An index for moderate- to high-functioning students, along with game descriptions for that population, follows the game descriptions for low-functioning students.

Table 5.4	Games-by-Skill-Level Index for Low-Functioning Students—Sitting Volleyball		
Skills	Individual activity	Small group activity	Teamwork
Passing	Table Target Pass I	Table Target Pass II	Table Target Pass III
Attack-hit	Tarzan Attack I	Tarzan Attack II	Tarzan Attack III
Block	Right Back at You	Roll and Block I	Keep It In
Serve	Serving Cone	Serving Line	Over It Goes

Game Descriptions

Each game description in this section includes game level, formation, equipment, description, extensions, and inclusion suggestions. These games are written with the idea of moving a student from an individual situation to a teamwork environment.

Skill Passing

◆ Table Target Pass I

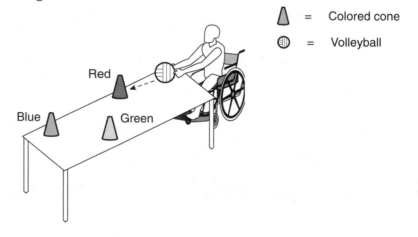

Game Level: Individual

Formation: The student is at one end of the table, and colored targets are at each of the three remaining sides of the table.

Equipment: Volleyball, small Nerf ball, or deflated playground ball; long folding table

Description: Students who have grip reach for a ball on the tabletop, lift the ball with two hands, return it to the tabletop, and roll it to a designated colored target (for example, a red cone or a blue beanbag).

Extension: Use one hand to simulate the bump pass.

Inclusion Suggestions: The student can demonstrate to the class their ability to accomplish the activity. The student can also select the order of passing, such as red target, then blue, then green.

◆ **Table Target Pass II**

Game Level: Small group

Formation: The student with a disability is at one end of the table and classmates (without disabilities) are at each of the three remaining sides.

Equipment: Small Nerf ball or deflated playground ball; long folding table

Description: Same concept as Table Target Passing I, except that the student passes the ball to their classmates. The passes should rotate from student to student around the table.

Extension: Students without disabilities should alternate at the table with others from the class.

Inclusion Suggestions: The student with a disability can decide how many times to pass the ball and must indicate that to those at the table. The student can also determine a change in order of passing and decide who should pass the ball first.

◆ **Table Target Pass III**

⬤ = Volleyball

┊ = Set

Game Level: Teamwork

Formation: Students without disabilities are in small circles around the gym, and the student with a disability is at a double-wide table (two tables side by side) with four or five students without disabilities at the table.

Equipment: Small Nerf ball or deflated playground ball; two long folding tables

Description: The game for the class is to use overhead passing and forearm passing to move the ball around the circle so that each person passes the ball using the two passes. The students at the table must do the same, except that they roll the ball to initiate the pass to their teammate. Once the ball reaches a teammate at the table, that student must pick the ball up from the table and complete one overhead pass to themselves, return the ball to the table, and pass it to another student who repeats the overhead self pass. Once everyone has passed the ball twice, the game is over.

Extensions: Students without disabilities can alternate overhead and forearm passes. Rotate a new team of students without disabilities at the table for each round you play the game.

Inclusion Suggestions: The student with a disability can decide which pass the team should perform first. The student can also determine who should start the game with the first pass.

Skill Attack-Hit

◆ Tarzan Attack I

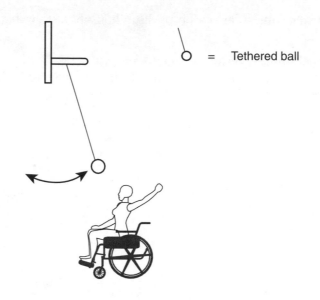

= Tethered ball

Game Level: Individual

Formation: The student is seated in a wheelchair under a ball that is tethered from a basketball rim so that it swings slightly above the student's head.

Equipment: Nerf volleyball, small Nerf ball, or deflated playground ball; rope for tethering; small net bag to hold the tethered ball

Description: On a signal, the ball is released so that it swings toward the student in a wheelchair. As the ball nears the student's overhead position, the student strikes or attack-hits the ball. The student may require physical assistance.

Extensions: Shorten the distance of the swing, use a larger ball, or use a beach ball.

Inclusion Suggestions: Students without disabilities can release the ball. The student with a disability can determine the distance to swing prior to the release of the tethered ball.

◆ Tarzan Attack II

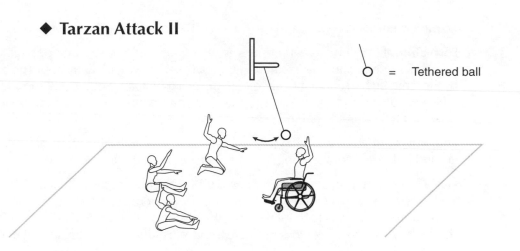

○ = Tethered ball

Game Level: Small group

Formation: Two to three students in a semicircle formation in front of the tethered ball from the basketball rim (See Tarzan Attack I)

Equipment: Nerf volleyball, small Nerf ball, or deflated playground ball; rope for tethering; small net bag to hold the tethered ball

Description: Students without disabilities are seated on the floor along with the student using a wheelchair; they are in a semicircle formation facing the tethered ball. On a signal, the ball is released so that it swings toward the students. As the ball nears a student's overhead position, they perform an attack-hit on the ball. Make sure to provide enough distance between students in the semicircle. The student with a disability may require physical assistance.

Extensions: Extend the number of hits to be made on the ball, use a larger ball, or use a beach ball.

Inclusion Suggestion: The student with a disability can release the ball on the initial swing.

◆ Tarzan Attack III

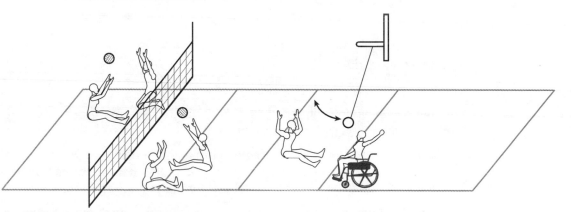

Game Level: Teamwork

Formation: Divide the class into teams with equal numbers. Place one team at each court; all students should be seated. The student using a wheelchair should be positioned by the tethered ball under the basketball rim near their team's court. It is important to pick a basketball rim that is adjacent to the volleyball courts. If this is not possible, other means of tethering the ball must be used.

Equipment: Regulation volleyball, Nerf volleyball, small Nerf ball, or deflated playground ball; rope for tethering; small net bag to hold the tethered ball

Description: The objective of the game is for each team to attack-hit a ball over the net. Each team gets two rounds before switching; the number of attack-hits that are grounded in the opponents' court are totaled. For the students without disabilities, the attack-hit should be set up by a high toss from a teammate. For the student using a wheelchair, the attack-hit is considered successful if that student strikes the swinging ball cleanly on each of two attempts. Minimal assistance should be provided during the hit; however, a student without a disability from the team should swing the ball forward.

Extension: Move the student with a disability to the court and attempt a toss and attack-hit combination using a slower-moving ball, such as a beach ball.

Inclusion Suggestion: The student with a disability can decide the number of successful attack-hits to complete for each team.

Skill Block

◆ Right Back at You
(from chapter 3, "Wheelchair Basketball," p. 36)

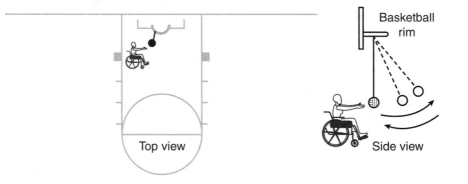

Game Level: Individual

Formation: Individual with peer assistant as needed

Equipment: Nerf volleyball, small Nerf ball, or deflated playground ball; rope for tethering; small net bag to hold the tethered ball

Description: A ball tethered to a basketball rim hangs at eye level for the student with a disability. The student pushes the ball away and blocks it as it returns from the push. Use student assistants on a recreational basis throughout the class session.

Extension: If grasp and release is an issue, physically assist, with emphasis on opening hands to receive the ball.

Inclusion Suggestion: The student with a disability can pick a partner to work with prior to moving to the small group activity.

◆ Roll and Block I

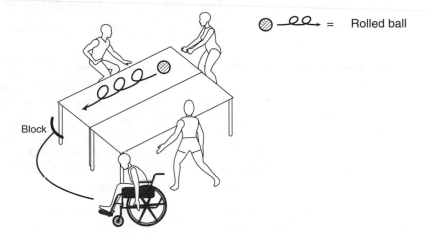

Block

🏐 ⟿ = Rolled ball

Game Level: Small group

Formation: Students without disabilities on each of three sides of two folding tables placed side by side and a student with a disability on the fourth side

Equipment: Nerf volleyball, small Nerf ball, or deflated playground ball; two folding tables placed side by side

Description: Allow the student with a wheelchair enough room to move their motorized wheelchair back and forth freely on their own table side. On a cue the students without disabilities release the ball across the table. The objective is to have the student using the wheelchair move quickly to block the ball from dropping off the table's edge. Students should roll the ball slowly enough to challenge the student using a wheelchair. The student with a disability should return to a neutral position at the table after each blocking attempt.

Extensions: Change the type of ball used; rotate new students to the table.

Inclusion Suggestion: The student with a disability can point to or indicate in some manner which student should roll the ball, rather than going in random order.

◆ Keep It In

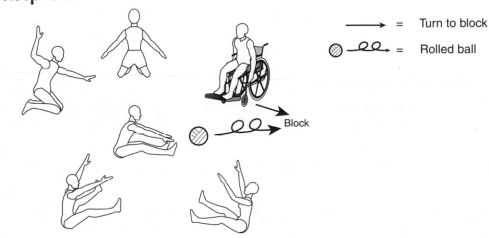

⟶ = Turn to block

🏐 ⟿ = Rolled ball

Block

Game Level: Teamwork

Formation: Divide the class into small groups and have the groups sit in circles around the gymnasium. Place one student without a disability in the center of the circle. The student using a wheelchair should be included in one of the circles.

Equipment: Regulation volleyball, Nerf volleyball, small Nerf ball, deflated playground ball, or large beach ball

Description: The student in the center of the circle, while seated, must attempt to pass the ball out of the circle using quick tosses. The objective is to have the students block the ball from exiting the circle. The tosses cannot be higher than arm's reach overhead, and blockers are allowed to use one or two arms to block. The student in the center makes five attempts. After five attempts, a new student takes the center position. When attempting to toss the ball out of the circle against the student using the wheelchair, the ball must be rolled on the floor. The student using a wheelchair must position their wheelchair quickly to block the ball from exiting the circle.

Extension: When the student using the wheelchair plays the center position, all students in the circle formation must sit with their backs to the middle. The student using a wheelchair must release a ball, with assistance as needed, and the students attempting to block the ball must listen carefully to the sound of the ball as it rolls toward them. They must block the ball without turning to watch where it has been rolled.

Inclusion Suggestion: The student with a disability can decide the distance of the circle's diameter when it is their turn to play the middle position.

Skill Serve

◆ Serving Cone

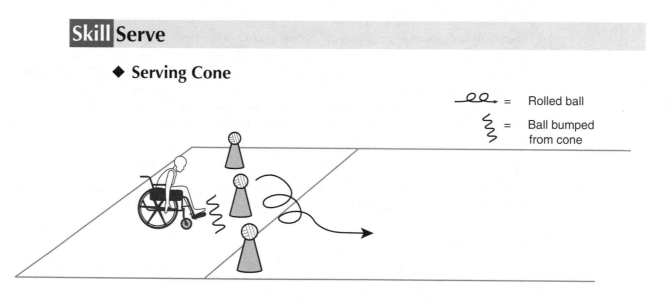

Game Level: Individual

Formation: Three tall traffic cones with volleyballs balanced on each and a student with a disability approximately three to four feet behind one of the cones

Equipment: Three tall traffic cones; regulation volleyballs, Nerf volleyballs, small Nerf balls, deflated playground balls, or large beach ball

Description: On a signal, the student using the wheelchair approaches the traffic cone and attempts to bump the cone so as to knock the ball from the top of the cone. As the ball is displaced from the cone, the serve is complete. The student repeats the movement for each of the remaining two traffic cones.

Extension: If the student has the functional ability, allow them to strike the ball with their hand or arm. Establish a distance the ball must travel after leaving the cone in order for the serve to be considered successful (for example, 10 feet).

Inclusion Suggestion: The student with a disability can decide the distance the ball must travel to be considered a successful serve.

◆ Serving Line

Game Level: Small group

Formation: Students without disabilities in a semicircle formation facing a student with a disability, who is positioned ready to serve a tethered ball

Equipment: Line or rope to tether the ball; regulation volleyball, Nerf volleyball, small Nerf ball, deflated playground ball, or large beach ball.

Description: The student with a disability is in front of the tethered ball, which should be stationary as it hangs from the basketball rim approximately four to five inches above the student's head. Two to three students without disabilities receive the serve in semicircle formation facing the server. On the signal, the student with a disability moves to strike the ball using an overhead serve motion with their arm. The student serves to all members of the group, then rotates out.

Extension: Students without disabilities can participate in this game from a seated position on the floor. Lower the tethered ball so that it hangs about four to five inches above their head and have them serve to the group using an overhead serve motion. Make sure to allow enough distance between the server and the group when the students without disabilities serve. Rotate students without disabilities through this game from members of the class.

Inclusion Suggestion: The student with a disability can decide the order of servers.

◆ Over It Goes

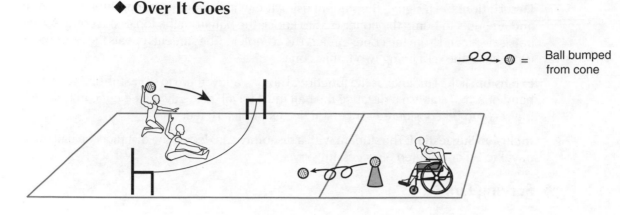

Ball bumped from cone

Game Level: Teamwork

Formation: Teams on the court, practicing serving from a seated position

Equipment: Regulation volleyball, Nerf volleyball, small Nerf ball, or large beach ball; volleyball net

Description: The class is divided into teams with each team situated on a separate court in a seated position. Place a net at regulation height, or use other material to create a net (for example, a rope strung across two folding chairs). Students without disabilities should practice overhead serving as described. The student with a disability should use the traffic cone from the Serving Cone game. Have the cone placed on the court with a volleyball balanced on top. A successful serve for the student with a disability occurs when the ball has been struck from the cone and rolls a predetermined distance, such as five feet. Each team should count successful serves within a given time period (three minutes). All teams should rotate to new courts every three minutes.

Extension: Move the student with a disability closer to the net and have them attempt to serve the ball up and over the net. You might consider using a beach ball to help increase ball trajectory.

Inclusion Suggestions: The student with a disability can determine the distance the ball should roll to be considered a successful serve. The student can also determine the number of times each team should serve before changing courts.

Games-by-Skill-Level Index: Moderate- to High-Functioning Students

The index in table 5.5 is designed to address those students with disabilities who are considered to have moderate to high function. The progression of activity suggestions remains the same: from individual, to small group, to teamwork. Descriptions of games for this population follow.

Table 5.5	Games-by-Skill-Level Index for Moderate- to High-Functioning Students—Sitting Volleyball		
Skills	Individual activity	Small group activity	Teamwork
Passing	Pass It Up	Up and Over I	Up and Over II
Attack-hit	Throw It Over I	Throw It Over II	Rip It
Block	Put 'em Up	The Wall	Just the Three of Us
Serve	Throw It Over I	Clean the Kitchen	Serving Math

Game Descriptions

The 12 games described in this section are specifically designed for students with moderate to high ability. As always, you should feel free to choose games appropriate to your unique physical education situation and population, as well as to modify any games as needed.

Skill Passing (Overhead and Forearm)

◆ Pass It Up

Game Level: Individual

Formation: Individual with peer assistant

Equipment: Regulation volleyball, Nerf volleyball, small Nerf ball, or large beach ball; rope for tethering; small net bag to hold the tethered ball

Description: The student with a disability and a partner are seated on the floor under a ball tethered to a basketball rim. The ball should hang between six and eight inches overhead. The student practices executing a correct overhead pass to their partner. After completing a predetermined number of overhead passes, the student with a disability practices forearm passes (bumps) to their partner. The tether will have to be lowered during the forearm passing activity.

Extension: The student can alternate on each pass with an overhead pass, then a forearm pass, and repeat for a predetermined number of passes.

Inclusion Suggestions: The student with a disability can demonstrate to the class their ability to accomplish the activity and decide how many passes to make before switching.

◆ Up and Over I

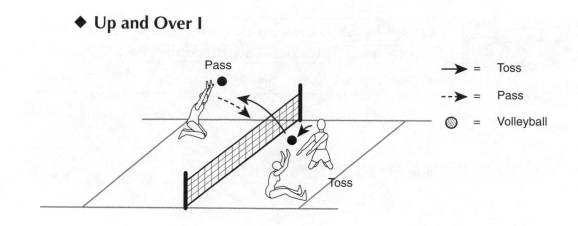

Game Level: Small group

Formation: Students in groups of three seated on each side of the net facing a partner

Equipment: Regulation volleyballs, Nerf volleyballs, or small Nerf balls; net.

Description: All students should be seated facing their partner across the net. Students work to pass the ball up and over the net to their partner. One student begins the activity with a "toss" of the ball to the student using an overhead pass. The toss must be high enough so that the passer can position underneath the ball as it descends. As the pass is made over the net, the receiving student attempts to pass it back using the same overhead passing technique. Groups attempt to make as many successful passes as possible in a given time.

Extensions: Change the location of the tosser to increase the distance to the passer. Rotate positions so that each student experiences tossing and passing.

Inclusion Suggestion: The student with a disability can determine which students should toss and pass for each rotation.

◆ Up and Over II

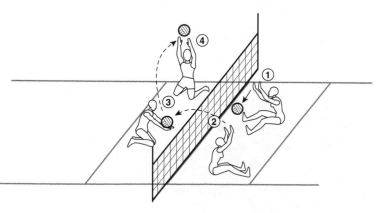

Game Level: Teamwork

Formation: Students in teams of three seated on each side of the net facing one another

Equipment: Regulation volleyballs, Nerf volleyballs, or small Nerf balls; net (Use a rope strung between two folding chairs if you don't have a net.)

Description: All students, those with and without disabilities, should be seated on both sides of the net facing the net. The game begins with a toss to the passer, who uses an overhead pass to move the ball to the opposite court. As the ball is received, the receiving student uses a forearm pass (bump) to their teammate, who in turn sends the ball back over the net using an overhead pass. The sequence should be "toss, overhead pass, forearm pass, overhead pass," ending with a catch by the original tosser. The objective of the game is to get as many complete cycles of this sequence for both teams in the time provided. The student with a disability is positioned on the floor with other students and must perform all skills (toss, overhead pass, and forearm pass).

Extensions: Attempt the game without the net first, then add the net if students are successful. Change the type of ball used if students are not successful with a regulation volleyball.

Inclusion Suggestion: The student with a disability can determine which students should toss and pass for each rotation.

Skill Attack-Hit

◆ Throw It Over I

Game Level: Individual

Formation: Individual with peer partner

Equipment: Regulation volleyball, Nerf volleyball, or small Nerf ball; net (Use a rope strung between two folding chairs if you don't have a net.)

Description: The student with a disability is seated on the floor facing the net. This is a simple game of throwing; the objective is to throw the ball over the net. Concentrate on teaching the student proper arm mechanics as they throw, since these mechanics are the same as those used to execute the attack-hit. The student should be positioned at a successful distance from the net.

Extensions: Change the distance to the net as the student becomes more successful with the game. A student without a disability can help to retrieve the balls thrown.

Inclusion Suggestions: The student with a disability can demonstrate their skill level if appropriate. The student can also teach a small group of students without disabilities the key points.

◆ **Throw It Over II**

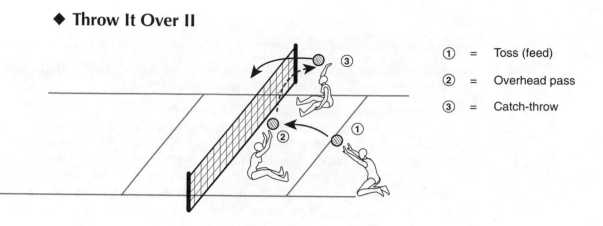

① = Toss (feed)

② = Overhead pass

③ = Catch-throw

Game Level: Small group

Formation: Small groups of three students seated on the floor in triangle formation

Equipment: Regulation volleyballs, Nerf volleyballs, or small Nerf balls; net. (Use a rope strung between two folding chairs if you don't have a net.)

Description: Students with and without disabilities participate in this activity. One student starts the activity with a toss, or "feed," to the second student. The second student passes the ball (overhead or set) up and close to the net for the third student, who catches the ball and throws it down to the opponents' court with force. The sequence should be "toss, pass, catch-throw." The objective is to make sure the passes are above and close to the net so that the catch-and-throw-down movement can be made forcefully. As skill levels improve, the students can begin to "attack-hit" the ball instead of catching and throwing, using the skill mechanics mentioned earlier in this chapter for the attack-hit.

Extensions: Students should rotate positions in the activity. Change the type of ball for the student with a disability if that student is not successful with the regulation volleyball.

Inclusion Suggestion: The student with a disability can decide the new positions and rotation for the group.

◆ **Rip It**

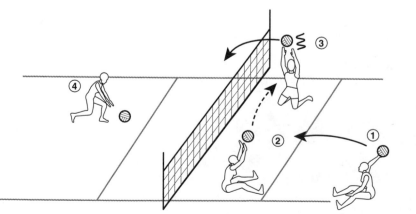

① = Toss (feed)

② = Pass (set)

③ = Hit

④ = Retriever

⧫ = Contact with ball

→ = Ball direction

Game Level: Teamwork

Formation: Students with and without disabilities are in triangle formation on the floor in teams of three or four. One student serves to retrieve the ball as needed.

Equipment: Regulation volleyballs, Nerf volleyballs, or small Nerf balls; net. (Use a rope strung between two folding chairs if you don't have a net.)

Description: The activity is very similar to Throw It Down II, with the exception that students are required to "attack-hit" the ball at the net. One student starts the activity with a toss, or "feed," to the second student. The second student passes the ball (overhead or set) up and close to the net for the third student, who attack-hits the ball to the opponents' court. There should be no attempt to block the attack-hit. The sequence is "toss, pass (set), hit." Each student should attempt to attack-hit at least once through three rotations.

Extensions: Students should rotate positions in the activity. Change the type of ball for the student with a disability if that student is not successful with the regulation volleyball.

Inclusion Suggestion: The student with a disability can decide one new combination or sequence to this activity (for example, "toss, pass (forearm), pass (set), hit").

Skill Block

◆ Put 'em Up

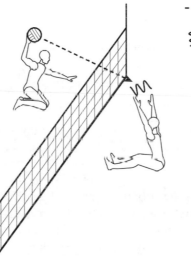

--→ = Tossed Ball

⌇ = Blocked ball

Game Level: Individual

Formation: Individual, seated in front of the net, working with a partner

Equipment: Regulation volleyball, Nerf volleyball, or small Nerf ball; net (Use a rope strung between two folding chairs if you don't have a net.)

Description: The student with a disability is seated in front of the volleyball net. A partner tosses a ball at the top of the net from the opposite side as the student with a disability attempts to put their arms and hands up to block the toss. The toss should be forceful and directed at the top of the net to simulate an attack-hit from an opponent.

Extension: Change the type of ball used if the student with a disability cannot move into position quickly enough to block or if the ball is too heavy and the student is at risk for injury.

Inclusion Suggestion: The student can demonstrate their skill level to the class after several sessions playing this game.

◆ The Wall

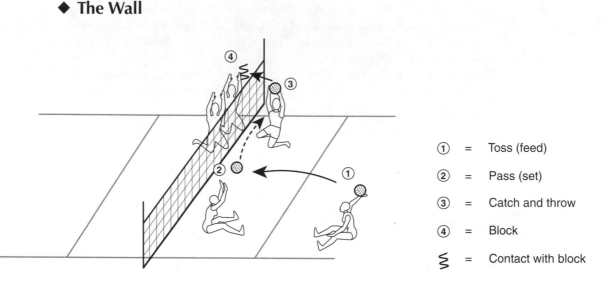

①	=	Toss (feed)
②	=	Pass (set)
③	=	Catch and throw
④	=	Block
⌇	=	Contact with block

Game Level: Small group

Formation: Small groups of two students in a side-by-side formation, while seated on the floor

Equipment: Regulation volleyballs, Nerf volleyballs, or small Nerf balls; net (Use a rope strung between two folding chairs if you don't have a net.)

Description: This is an extension of Throw It Over II and should be played by students with and without disabilities. The objective of this game is to have two students side by side form a "wall" and attempt to block the throw-over. As the throw-over is made, two students on the opposite side of the net block the throw by positioning themselves in a blocking stance as described earlier in this chapter. The emphasis here is on the position of both students, who should be side by side with arms extended overhead and hands held together. Timing is the key to this game, as the students must learn to move into the blocking position as the ball is being readied for the throw-over.

Extension: Change the type of ball to block for the student with a disability if the ball being used presents a risk of injury.

Inclusion Suggestion: The student with a disability can decide how many blocks are made for each small-group rotation.

◆ Just the Three of Us

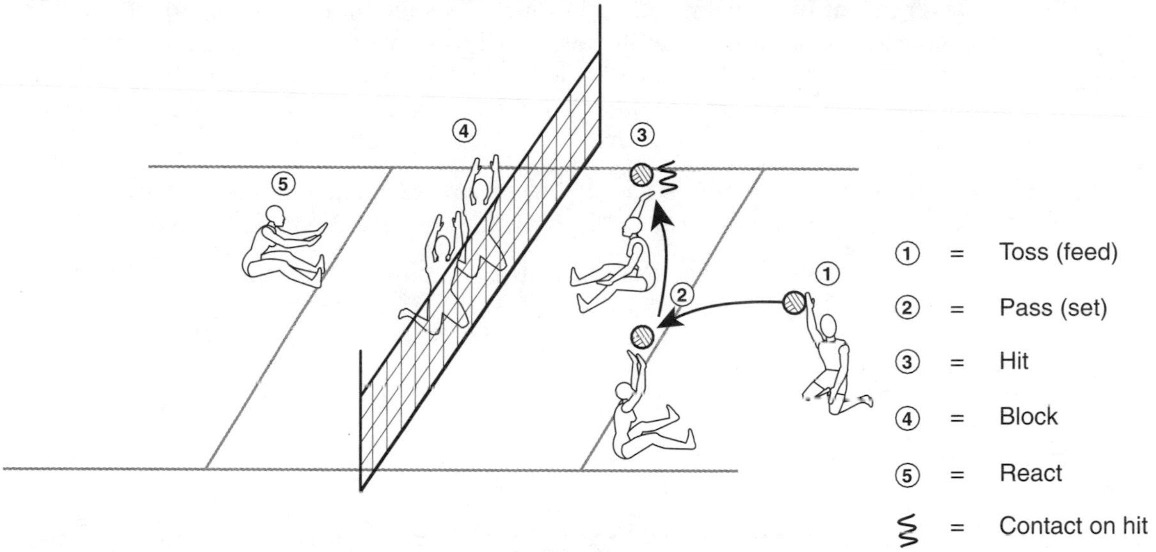

① = Toss (feed)

② = Pass (set)

③ = Hit

④ = Block

⑤ = React

§ = Contact on hit

Game Level: Teamwork

Formation: Small groups of three students seated on the floor in a triangle

Equipment: Regulation volleyballs, Nerf volleyballs, or small Nerf balls; net (Use a rope strung between two folding chairs if you don't have a net.)

Description: This is an extension of Rip It and should be played by students with and without disabilities. In the game Rip It, students practice the sequence of pass, set, and attack-hit. In this game, a set of blockers is added on the opposite side of the net. The block is made by two of the three students positioned at the net in a blocking position. The third student is positioned behind and to the side of the blockers, ready to react to the rebound of the block. If the ball is blocked and it rebounds to the same side of the court, the third student must react in an attempt to pass the ball up for their teammates. If the ball is blocked back to the opponents' court, the third student changes places with one of the blockers for the next attack-hit. The activity continues until all students have played each of the three positions.

Extension: Change the type of ball to block for the student with a disability if the ball being used presents a risk of injury.

Inclusion Suggestion: The student with a disability can decide who starts at the net for blocking and who is positioned as the third student on the team.

Skill Serve

◆ Throw It Over I

Game Level: Individual

Formation: Individual with peer partner

Equipment: Regulation volleyball, Nerf volleyball, or small Nerf ball; net (Use a rope strung between two folding chairs if you don't have a net.)

Description: The student with a disability is seated on the floor facing the net. This is a simple throwing game; the objective is to throw the ball over the net. The student should concentrate on proper arm mechanics as they throw, since these mechanics are the same as those used in the serve. Student should be positioned at a successful distance from the net.

Extensions: Change the distance to the net as the student becomes more successful with the game. A student without a disability can retrieve the balls thrown.

Inclusion Suggestion: The student with a disability can demonstrate their skill level if appropriate.

◆ Clean the Kitchen

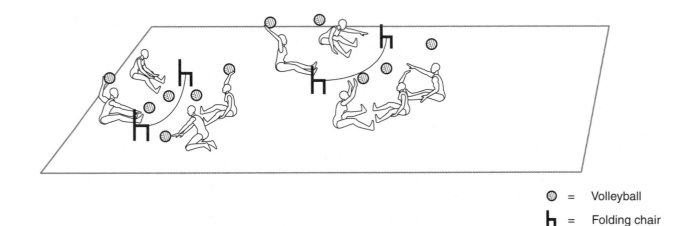

⊕ = Volleyball

h = Folding chair

Game Level: Small group

Formation: Small groups positioned on each side of the net. If you set up three nets, you will have six groups (one group on each side). At least one student per court can retrieve and then rotate into the game. Students with and without disabilities participate in this activity.

Equipment: Regulation volleyballs, Nerf volleyballs, or small Nerf balls; net

Description: Start the activity with an equal number of balls on the each side of the net(s). On the signal, the students must attempt to serve the ball over the net to their opponents' court and "keep their kitchen clean." As the ball is received into the court, that team must return it as soon as possible in the same attempt to keep their kitchen clean. The objective is to have the least number of balls in your court (kitchen) when the whistle blows. The only method of ball movement is serving; students are not allowed to throw or pass the ball over to the opposite court (kitchen). One student on each court retrieves errant balls, since everyone participating is seated. The student retriever is rotated as each new game is started.

Extension: Eliminate the net until students' skill levels improve.

Inclusion Suggestion: The student with a disability can suggest one variation to this activity (for example, changing the number of balls on each court).

◆ Serving Math

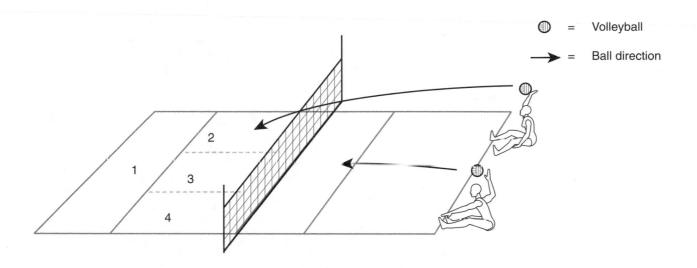

Game Level: Teamwork

Formation: Teams of three to five students with and without disabilities, seated on the floor

Equipment: Regulation volleyballs, Nerf volleyballs, or small Nerf balls; net (Use a rope strung between two folding chairs if you don't have a net.)

Description: Divide the court into three sections and give each section a numerical value. The values can be any combination of numbers you desire. Position the teams at the serving lines of their respective courts. The objective of the game is to reach a predetermined number (for example, 22) by serving the ball into the correct numerical sections of the opponents' court. Each member must practice serving while attempting to reach the designated value. As the teacher you may present the problem as an addition, subtraction, multiplication, or division problem. For example, you might say, "Divide the number 100 by 10 and serve into the correct sections until your team gets the correct answer." The students would then try to serve into their opponents' court until they reached a total of 10. If the problem cannot be answered by serving, have the students come as close as possible without going over the value.

Extension: Change the sections to a series of colors and tell the class to serve the ball in a particular sequence (for example, blue-red-green or red-green-blue). Make each section of the court a state and present them with geography problems (for instance, "Which state is closest to the Atlantic Ocean?").

Inclusion Suggestions: The student with a disability can suggest a topic for the court sections (for example, favorite basketball teams, famous musicians).

chapter

6

Wheelchair Tennis

The history of wheelchair tennis in the United States can be traced to three key individuals, Brad Parks, Randy Snow, and Dr. Bal Moore. Each of these individuals has contributed to the sport at the local, national, collegiate, and international levels of competition.

Brad Parks had been an athlete prior to his spinal cord injury in the mid-1970s. During a family vacation he began to experiment with wheelchair tennis and soon found success with the sport. Parks is credited with developing the two bounce rule and, along with his therapist David Saltz, establishing the National Foundation of Wheelchair Tennis in 1979.

Randy Snow and Dr. Bal Moore teamed up to become perhaps the greatest player–coach combination ever to grace the wheelchair tennis world. Snow was injured in a farming accident at the age of 16, and Moore redirected his basketball coaching career to make himself one of the leading tennis instruction professionals in the world. Snow and Moore met in 1989 at the Lakeshore Rehabilitation Hospital in Birmingham, Alabama. Snow was conducting a wheelchair tennis camp at Lakeshore when he caught Moore's eye. Moore, then head tennis coach at Jefferson State Community College, noted Snow's athleticism and invited him to practice with the college team. Intrigued with wheelchair tennis, Moore began to apply his kinesiology and biomechanics education to the sport. As the friendship between the two men grew, so did their professional relationship and in the early 1990's they established the World Wheelchair Tennis Academy in Rhinelander, Wisconsin. Together they teamed up to win wheelchair tennis titles at the 1990 World Games for the Disabled and at the 1992 and 1996 Paralympics. Moore did not participate in the 2000 Paralympics in Sydney. Snow competed but lost to the eventual men's singles champion 6-4, 7-5 in the early rounds.

Wheelchair tennis in America has grown from its humble beginnings in the 1970s to over 55 sanctioned tournaments and more than 2,000 competitors by 1986. In 1992, wheelchair tennis was officially recognized as a medal sport at the Barcelona Paralympics. According to the 2001 International Tennis Foundation (ITF) Web site (www.itftennis.com), over 330 men and 100 women from around the world are ranked in singles competition. In Barcelona, more than 48 players, 32 men and 16 women, from 16 countries competed in international competition. As of this writing the ITF and the United States Tennis Association (USTA) recognize wheelchair tennis as an integral part of their programs.

Description of the Sport

Wheelchair tennis is very similar to tennis played by individuals without disabilities. The game is played on the same regulation court, using the same boundary lines and markings. There are competition categories for men and women in singles and doubles, plus a mixed category. The game is started with a serve that must bounce within the opponent's court. The most noticeable difference between wheelchair tennis and regulation tennis is that two bounces are allowed before the player must return the ball during a rally.

Field of Play

The game is played on a regulation court measuring 78 feet long and 36 feet wide for doubles and 27 feet wide for singles. The net is 3 feet high, and the doubles alleys are 4 feet 6 inches wide. The singles serving court is 13 feet 6 inches wide and 26 feet long.

Players

Any person medically diagnosed as having a mobility-related disability is eligible to play wheelchair tennis. Individuals commonly identified with the sport might have one of the following limitations: spinal cord injury (paraplegic or quadriplegic), polio, spina bifida, or cerebral palsy. This list of conditions is not meant to be all inclusive, however; students with other mobility limitations can be eligible to play wheelchair tennis.

Equipment

A player's wheelchair is considered part of the player's body. The game is played with a regulation size racket and official USTA tennis balls.

Starting the Game

The game is started with a serve. The server must have all wheels of their wheelchair behind the baseline during the serve. The server must remain stationary during the serve and is not allowed to roll into the serve or adjust their wheelchair position to gain an advantage. The small wheels (casters) are not allowed to be over the baseline in the court area during the serve.

Game Objective

The objective of the game is to serve the ball in such a manner as to not allow your opponent to have a successful return. If the service return is successful and a rally ensues, players continue to rally the ball until one player fails to return the ball successfully. Unsuccessful returns in wheelchair tennis are those returned after more than two bounces, returns sent out of bounds, or returns not sent over the net.

In doubles competition, the same objective exists. Each player from a team serves a game during their turn. The right to serve remains with a team until a ball is not returned legally by the serving team; at that time the serve is given to the other team. When the serve is awarded back to the original team, the second member of the team has the opportunity to serve. This rotation continues throughout the game.

A player's success in wheelchair tennis depends on their functional ability and wheelchair mobility skills. The majority of play for the beginner happens deep in the court area, behind the baseline. Players will have much more success if they are taught to play deeper in the court. Remember, in wheelchair tennis the ball is allowed to bounce twice, and only one of the bounces must be within the boundaries of the court area. The second bounce can occur outside the boundary lines and is still considered eligible for play.

The area of the court that has the second most frequent rallies is between the baseline and the service line. This is usually the area where the ball bounces once, thus forcing the player to make a decision about hitting a quick return for a "winner." Rally play in this area requires a student to have very good wheelchair skills (reverse mobility) and an above-average command of several tennis strokes (for example, the top-spin forehand and the backhand slice).

The third area of the court is between the net and the service line; it is the forwardmost area on the court. This area should be addressed by more advanced players. Rally points addressed from this area usually end with the player attempting to end the point. The player must have excellent wheelchair and racket control to rally a ball from this area.

The skills mentioned in this chapter and the games suggested are for beginners and not advanced players. Students with disabilities and those without, who are learning wheelchair tennis for the first time should practice their play from behind the baseline. As they develop in skill and wheelchair mobility, they can play closer to the net.

Game Length

Wheelchair tennis follows USTA rules regarding game, set, and match length. Scoring is the same for a game (love, 15, 30, 40, deuce, advantage, and game), and it takes six games to win a set. If two players have each won five games, then the set is continued until a player has won by two games. A player must win three sets in official men's competition and two sets in women's competition to be declared the match winner.

General Rules/Penalties

As mentioned, all the rules in regulation tennis apply to wheelchair tennis, with the exception of a few that are specific to the game.

Rules Specific to Wheelchair Tennis

The most visible rule change specific to wheelchair tennis is the two-bounce rule. The players are allowed two bounces to return a ball to the opponent's court. Keep in mind that only the first bounce has to be inside the court's boundary lines.

When serving the ball, all wheels must remain behind the baseline. The player serving the ball may not change positions throughout the serve by rolling or spinning their wheels. If a player uses any part of their body to stabilize or stop their wheelchair during service delivery, the serve will be considered a fault. A player is allowed to use unconventional methods to initiate the serve due to physical limitations (e.g., a second person may drop the ball to the server).

The wheelchair is considered part of the player's body along with anything that is carried on the wheelchair. If a ball touches the wheelchair or anything carried on the wheelchair (besides the player's racket) during a rally, it is considered a loss of point. Likewise, in doubles competition if a player hits their partner during the serve or a rally, it is considered a fault and results in the loss of a point.

During a rally, if a player uses their feet to stop, change directions, or turn their wheelchair, it is considered a fault and the player loses a point. Also, the player must maintain contact with the seat of the wheelchair with at least one buttock during a rally. A player is allowed to fall from the wheelchair, get back in unassisted, and complete a rally without penalty.

Tournament directors may enforce rules to assure court protection from damages by wheelchairs. Players may be asked to pad footplates and secure antitip devices behind their wheelchairs.

Summary of the Sport

Table 6.1 is a summary of wheelchair tennis. Use it as a quick reference to the sport.

Table 6.1	Overview of Wheelchair Tennis
Field of play	Tennis court: 78 ft by 36 ft for doubles; 78 ft by 27 ft for singles
Players	Singles and doubles competition
Equipment	Regulation tennis court and net Regulation tennis racket and tennis balls
Legal start	The game is started with a serve.
Ball movement	Players rally the ball using rackets. Players are allowed two bounces before the ball must be returned during a rally. The first of the two bounces must be within the boundaries of the tennis court. A player may not touch the playing surface while in possession of the ball.

	A player may receive assistance during a serve if physical limitations restrict the movement, for example, someone may drop the ball in front of the player in preparation to serve.
Rally play	Serving must take place behind the baseline with all wheels off the court markings. Rally play becomes more difficult and requires greater skill level the closer the student plays to the net. The objective is to move the opponent out of position so as not to allow a safe rally return.
Faults	Points are lost if: • the ball strikes the player or any part of the wheelchair during a serve or rally play; • the ball strikes anything carried on the wheelchair, except the racket during rally play; • in doubles, the ball strikes the partner during a serve or rally play; or • a player uses their feet to stop, change directions, or turn their wheelchair during play.

Skills to Be Taught

Two areas of skill development should be addressed in wheelchair tennis: wheelchair mobility and tennis skills. Wheelchair mobility skills are at the core of success for a competitive wheelchair tennis player. So as not to overlook these important skills, please review the information presented in chapter 2, "Wheelchair Basics," regarding propelling, stopping, and turning a wheelchair. All of these skills are crucial in wheelchair tennis.

This chapter is focused on the three tennis skills associated with striking the ball: the forehand, the backhand, and the serve. Because these are likely the same skills you teach to students without disabilities during your tennis unit, wheelchair tennis is a logical game to help you with inclusion.

Because tennis is an individual sport rather than a team sport, it is somewhat easier to include students with and without disabilities in the same unit. Unlike wheelchair basketball, in which you might need several wheelchairs to play, with wheelchair tennis you need only one additional wheelchair to create a game or activity.

As you have read in previous chapters, you must be able to assess your students' functional ability to play wheelchair tennis. Remember, you can modify several aspects of the game, such as racket and ball size, net height, and court dimensions, to make this sport appropriate for your students with disabilities.

Grip

In traditional tennis, the type of grip used is not directly related to the player's ability to move about the court. In wheelchair tennis, however, there is an extremely important interface between racket grip and wheelchair mobility.

Because in wheelchair tennis the player must hold the racket while pushing the wheelchair, the correct racket grip is paramount to the player's performance. The player must choose a grip that combines racket control with wheelchair mobility.

The grip considered to be the most versatile is the eastern grip. The eastern grip is described as "shaking hands with the racket." The skills mentioned in this chapter will assume that the player is using the eastern grip.

Eastern grip for wheelchair mobility.

Forehand

To execute a forehand from the baseline on a ball hit directly at the player, the player must pull back on the dominant wheel first in preparation for the stroke. As the ball nears, the player pulls back on the nondominant wheel and positions the racket back in preparation to strike the ball. The racket should be held with an extended arm, and the dominant shoulder should be rotated away from the net. At contact, the player swings forward and pulls harder on the nondominant wheel. This combination of striking the forehand and pulling on the nondominant wheel helps turn the player into the shot. Turning into the shot adds additional power to the forehand stroke.

Pull back with the nondominant hand and prepare to hit forehand.

Turn into the shot during ball contact.

Backhand

To execute a backhand shot on a ball hit directly at the player, the player may want to turn into the ball as the stroke is made. To execute turning into a backhand shot, the player must develop a cross-hand turn prior to striking the ball. To execute the cross-hand turn, the player reaches across the wheelchair with the nondominant arm and grabs the dominate wheel. The player needs to stabilize their body by pressing the forearm of the nondominant arm against the thigh on the dominant side. As the nondominant arm is held in this position, the wheelchair should start to turn into the

Use the cross-hand turn to prepare for a backhand; the forearm presses on the thigh and the striking arm is drawn back.

oncoming ball and position the player to strike with a backhand stroke. Once in position to strike the ball, the backhand is executed with the same back-to-forward motion taught in regulation tennis. The racket should be drawn back to a point close to the opposite hip, and the elbow should be slightly flexed. The player turns into the shot and makes contact with the ball, remembering to keep their wrist firm during the follow-through.

Use the nondominant arm to turn into position for a backhand stroke.

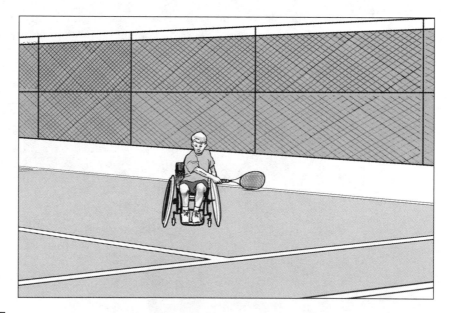

Move forward and strike with a firm wrist.

Serve

The types of serves used in wheelchair tennis include the top-spin, slice, modified slice, reverse cut, and kick serve. However, because this chapter is written with the beginning wheelchair tennis player in mind, only the top-spin serve will be discussed.

The key to all serves is coordinating turning the wheelchair with making contact with the ball. To help with this skill, it is important to position the wheelchair behind the baseline and turn it at a 45-degree angle to the net. Positioning the wheelchair slightly behind the baseline allows the player to turn into the serve and not allow the front casters to cross the baseline during the serve.

Turned 45 degrees away from the net, the player starts the serving motion with both arms straight and slightly down. To initiate the service movement, both arms rise simultaneously until the ball is ready to be tossed. The player should toss the ball as their hand reaches head height or slightly higher. The racket continues to rise and be pulled back behind the head in preparation to strike the ball. As the ball is tossed, the nondominant hand must return immediately to the front wheel as the striking arm continues backward in preparation to be moved forward. As the tossed ball reaches its apex and begins to descend, the nondominant hand must pull back on the front wheel, generating a turn or rotational movement. This turning movement is analogous to the hip and shoulder rotation seen during the tennis serve in individuals without disabilities. The ball is struck with an extended arm and pronated forearm above the front casters of the wheelchair. As the serve is made, the nondominant hand continues to pull backward helping to increase the power applied to the serve. Once contact is made, the dominant arm continues down and across the body for follow-through, and in preparation to move the wheelchair in anticipation of the opponent's service return.

Position at the baseline: the wheelchair is turned 45 degrees and the toss is released at head height.

The nondominant hand returns to the front wheel after the toss.

Serve the ball with an extended arm and firm wrist.

Functional Profiles and General Modifications

Table 6.2 suggests student profiles that might fit your teaching situation. Remember, this book is about helping you to make sound pedagogical decisions while using your personal creativity. Read the table to see if you have students that might fit these profiles. Then consider the activity modifications listed in table 6.3.

Student Functional Profiles

Much of the student's success in wheelchair tennis depends on their ability to hold the racket and manually move the wheelchair. Functional profiles for this sport will focus on the levels of assistance needed to help the student grip the tennis racket. These functional profiles are operationally defined using a variation of the classification system employed by several disability sport organizations, including the National Wheelchair Basketball Association, the National Disability Sports Alliance, Disabled Sports USA, and Wheelchair Sports USA. For the purposes of this book, it is not important that you precisely classify your students with disabilities. Rather, these profiles are merely suggestions to help you begin more appropriate physical education programming.

Table 6.2	Student Functional Profiles for Wheelchair Tennis
Functional skill level	**Student profile**
Low	Multiple impairments; unable to manually maneuver a wheelchair; needs assistance positioning in wheelchair; needs assistance holding a racket; might use a power wheelchair
Moderate	Able to maneuver a manual wheelchair independently for short distances; can hold a racket independently with one hand; has moderate active range of motion and independent sitting posture
High	Able to maneuver a manual wheelchair independently for longer distances (30-50 ft); can hold a racket independently with one hand and maneuver the wheelchair simultaneously; has high active range of motion in upper body and independent sitting posture; can move continuously for 10 min without stopping.

General Modifications

Table 6.3 offers suggestions for general modifications that you might use when teaching wheelchair tennis to your students with disabilities. These modifications are meant as general overviews and are not specific to a student's functional profile. You can decide how to apply these modifications to your unique student population.

Table 6.3	General Modifications for Wheelchair Tennis	
Skill level	**Skill**	**Activity modifications**
Low	Forehand/ Backhand	Use modified or lightweight racket (e.g., badminton) to strike a suspended ball for all three skills. Use elastic bandage to wrap racket to hand. Use lightweight butterfly net to catch tossed Nerf balls.
	Serve	Attach lightweight racket to armrest of wheelchair and strike a suspended ball while turning the entire wheelchair.
Moderate	Forehand/ Backhand	Use semi-lightweight racket (e.g., racquetball) to strike a suspended ball for all three skills. Use larger balls for striking (e.g., 4-in. playground ball).
	Serve	Reduce the distance to be served.
High	All skills	No modifications: Used with highest-functioning students.

Game Progressions

As you use the activities and games presented in the following section, keep in mind that you are trying to support inclusion of all three learning domains (psychomotor, cognitive, and affective). The progression sequence of the activities is the same as in previous chapters (individual, to small group, to teamwork).

Games-by-Skill-Level Index: Low-Functioning Students

Table 6.4 presents an index of activities for low-functioning students that are cross-referenced to the skills you may want to address in your physical education class. For low-functioning students, it is probably helpful to start with individual activities before moving on to small group and teamwork situations. Refer back to table 6.2 to help you decide the level of function of your students with disabilities. This will help you determine whether to use the activities in this section or those in the section for moderate- to high-functioning students that follows.

Table 6.4	Games-by-Skill-Level Index for Low-Functioning Students—Wheelchair Tennis		
Skills	**Individual activity**	**Small group activity**	**Teamwork**
Forehand	Strike It Rich I	Tabletop Tennis	Tarzan Tennis
Backhand	Strike It Rich II	Balloon Backhand	Zigzag Tennis
Serve	Strike It Rich III	Delivery Service	Guest Server

Game Descriptions

From the games that follow, feel free to select any game that you feel matches the ability level of your students with mobility impairments. As mentioned, these games are written with the idea of moving a student from an individual situation to a teamwork environment.

Skill Forehand

◆ Strike It Rich I

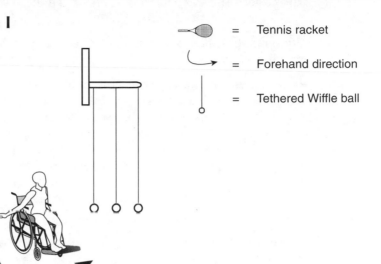

= Tennis racket

= Forehand direction

= Tethered Wiffle ball

Game Level: Individual

Formation: Individual with a peer assistant

Equipment: Wiffle ball, rope or cord for tether, modified racket

Description: Tether several Wiffle balls with thin rope or cord from a basketball rim or some overhead support so that they hang approximately at sitting height. Space the suspended balls about three feet apart. The student with a disability is at an angle that allows them to turn their wheelchair into the suspended ball as they perform a forehand shot. For example, if the student is right-handed, the ball would hang closer to the left side of the wheelchair. To perform the forehand stroke, the student turns the wheelchair sharply to the left (counterclockwise) bringing the racket around to strike the ball.

Extensions: Set up three or four forehand striking stations around the gymnasium and have the student move from one to the other. The student can start the activity using only their hand to strike.

Inclusion Suggestion: The student can decide how and when to rotate stations.

◆ Tabletop Tennis

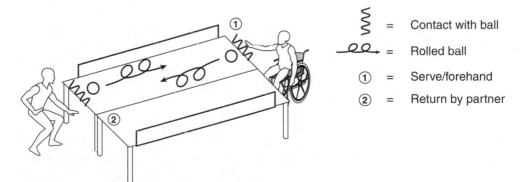

= Contact with ball

= Rolled ball

① = Serve/forehand

② = Return by partner

Game Level: Small group

Formation: The student is at one end of a double-wide tabletop, and a partner is at the opposite end. A third student should be used to help retrieve errant forehand strokes.

Equipment: Beach ball, beanbag, two folding tables, modified rackets (badminton), cardboard panels

Description: The student with a disability is at one end of the table in the ready position to execute a forehand stroke. A beach ball is on the end of the table closest to the student, balanced on the beanbag to help keep the ball stationary. A student without a disability is at the opposite end of the table ready to return the ball. Using a forearm motion, the student with a disability strikes the ball toward the opposite end of the table, then prepares for the return stroke. The student acting as a retriever should help reposition the ball after it has been hit. The objective is to have the beach ball roll down the table to the opponent. Cardboard panels set up on each side of the table can help keep the ball from rolling off the side edge.

Extensions: Use a heavier ball (playground, Nerf, deflated volleyball) if the beach ball does not work. A racquetball racket can also be used in place of the badminton racket. Rotate the student retrieving with the student returning the forehand stroke and make sure to rotate all classmates through this activity during class time. The student may strike using only their hand.

Inclusion Suggestions: The student with a disability can change ends of the table when they are ready. The student may also be allowed to choose the size and type of ball to use.

◆ Tarzan Tennis

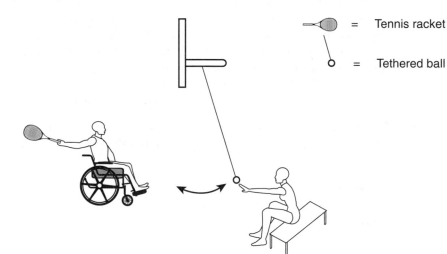

= Tennis racket

= Tethered ball

Game Level: Teamwork

Formation: The student with a disability is in front of a suspended ball as in the game Strike It Rich I (p. 137). A classmate is opposite this student seated in a folding chair or on a bench ready to return the ball. The student should be far enough away to allow a safe swing with the racket. Rotate students without disabilities from the class into the activity during the class session.

Equipment: Wiffle ball, rope or cord for tether, modified racket, folding chair

Description: Tether a Wiffle ball with thin rope or cord from a basketball rim or some overhead support so that it hangs at sitting height. The student without a disability should hold the ball far enough away to create a pendulum swing of the ball toward the student with a disability. The student with a disability should be at an angle that allows them to turn their wheelchair into the swinging ball to perform the forehand shot (counterclockwise turn for right-handers). As the ball approaches, the student with a disability must time the swing of the ball and use a forehand stroke to send the ball back in the direction of their opponent. The objective of the game is to complete a designated number of successive forehand strokes without missing (e.g., five forehands).

Extension: Change the size, weight, or height of the suspended ball as needed.

Inclusion Suggestion: The student with a disability can decide how many forehands will be hit before the game ends.

Skill Backhand

◆ **Strike It Rich II**

$\longleftarrow$ = Backhand direction

| = Tethered ball

Game Level: Individual

Formation: Same formation as Strike It Rich I using a peer assistant

Equipment: Wiffle ball, rope or cord for tether, modified racket

Description: Tether several Wiffle balls with thin rope or cord from a basketball rim or some overhead support so that they hang approximately at sitting height. Space the suspended balls about three feet apart. The student with a disability should be at an angle that allows them to turn their wheelchair into the suspended ball as they perform a backhand shot. For example, if the student is right-handed, the ball would hang closer to the right side of the wheelchair. To perform the backhand stroke, the student turns the wheelchair sharply to the right (clockwise) bringing the racket around to strike the ball.

Extension: Set up three or four forehand striking stations around the gymnasium and have the student move from one to the other.

Inclusion Suggestion: The student can decide how and when to rotate stations.

◆ Balloon Backhand

Game Level: Small group

Formation: The student with a disability is in the middle of a circle formation.

Equipment: Balloons, modified rackets (badminton)

Description: Each student has a balloon. As the student with a disability turns to face each student, that student tosses their balloon in the air to free float toward the student in the middle. The objective is to have the student with a disability position their wheelchair to execute a backhand stroke and send the balloon out of the circle. The student with a disability moves around the circle to address each student with a balloon. The game is over when all balloons have been tossed.

Extensions: Make the circle wider and use medium-sized Nerf balls instead of balloons. Bounce the balls into the center of the circle and have the student with a disability backhand the ball after two bounces.

Inclusion Suggestions: The student with a disability can decide the size of the circle and the object to be tossed or bounced into the middle. The student can also decide who moves to the center next.

◆ Zigzag Tennis

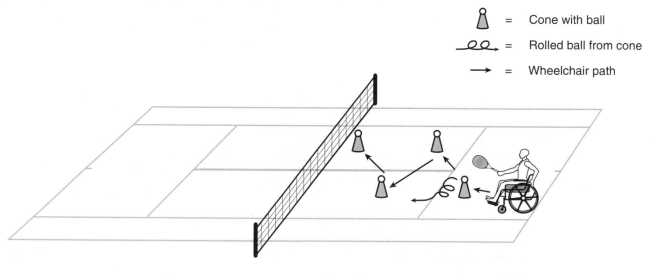

🔺	=	Cone with ball
〰️	=	Rolled ball from cone
→	=	Wheelchair path

Game Level: Teamwork

Formation: Three- to four-person teams

Equipment: Tall traffic cones, tennis balls, modified racket, tennis court (indoor or outdoor)

Description: The students without disabilities are divided into three-person teams. The objective of the game is to have one teammate bounce the ball to a second teammate, who sends it over the net using a backhand stroke to a third teammate, who catches it. Once the third teammate has secured four tennis balls, they must run to exchange positions with their teammates. The retriever becomes the feeder, the feeder becomes the backhand striker, and the backhand striker becomes the retriever.

To include the student with a disability in this game, assist the student with gripping the racket as needed or secure the racket to the wheelchair if appropriate. Place four tall traffic cones on the tennis court in a zigzag pattern. Balance a tennis ball on each traffic cone. On the signal, start the student with a disability from the centerline/baseline intersect. The objective is to have the student move to each cone and strike the ball from the cone using a backhand stroke. The student should move from one side of the court to the opposite side as they move to strike the tennis balls. The feeder and the retriever place the balls on the traffic cones.

Extensions: Increase the distance between the traffic cones; attempt to bounce-feed the student with a disability for a backhand stroke.

Inclusion Suggestion: The student can decide where to place the traffic cones or how many traffic cones to use.

Skill Serve

◆ Strike It Rich III

Game Level: Individual

Formation: Individual with a peer assistant

Equipment: Wiffle ball, rope or cord for tether, modified racket

Description: Tether several Wiffle balls with thin rope or cord from a basketball rim or some overhead support so that they hang approximately at sitting height. Space the suspended balls about three feet apart. The student with a disability should be at an angle that allows them to turn their wheelchair into the suspended ball as they perform a serve. For example, if the student is right-handed, the ball would hang closer to the left side of the wheelchair. To perform the serve, the student turns the wheelchair sharply to the left (counterclockwise) bringing the racket around to strike the ball.

Extension: Set up three or four serving stations around the gymnasium and have the student move from one to the other.

Inclusion Suggestion: The student can decide how and when to rotate stations.

◆ Delivery Service

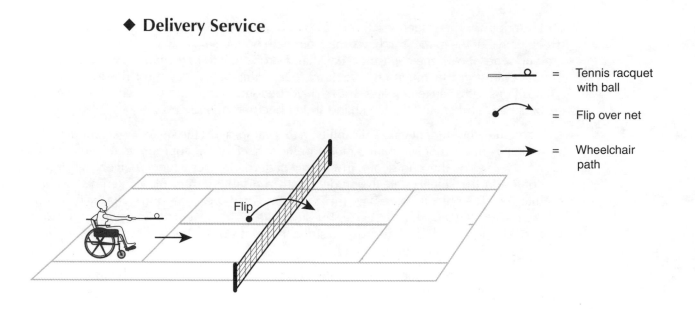

	=	Tennis racquet with ball
	=	Flip over net
	=	Wheelchair path

Flip

Game Level: Small group

Formation: Students are in groups of two or three at the baseline.

Equipment: Modified rackets, tennis rackets, beanbags, small Nerf balls, tennis balls

Description: Students without disabilities are at the baseline and practicing serving the ball using the teachings cues from your lesson. For the student with a disability, assist with racket grip as needed (Velcro strap or elastic wraps to either their hand or wheelchair armrest). Position the racket face up, level, and parallel with the court surface. Balance a beanbag on the racket face and instruct the student to deliver the beanbag to the net by moving the wheelchair forward. Once at the net, instruct the student to flip the racket and serve the beanbag to the opponent's court. Repeat the activity as needed for the time allotted.

Extensions: Change the object carried on the racket; for example, use a Nerf ball or a tennis ball. Increase the distance from the net to the delivery, and have the student serve the object from farther away.

Inclusion Suggestions: Challenge each group to get as many serves into the opponent's court as possible in the time available, and rotate the student with a disability through each group. The student with a disability can be responsible for reporting the number of serves for each group.

◆ Guest Server

Game Level: Teamwork

Formation: The class is divided into doubles teams and positioned at the courts

Equipment: Modified rackets, tennis rackets, beanbags, small Nerf balls, tennis balls

Description: The class will play doubles tennis, and the student with a disability will be the guest server for at least one game on every court. The student with a disability is the guest long enough to bring the ball to the net in order to simulate a serve. The objective is to have the student with a disability move from court to court and serve the ball as described in the game Delivery Service. To serve, the student with a disability balances the ball on their racket and travels to the net to flip the ball over the net to serve. If the serve is successful, play is stopped momentarily while the ball is retrieved. During that time the student with a disability exits the court, and the team who received the serve continues play with a forehand ground stroke. As play continues on the first court, the student with a disability travels to the next court and waits for a service break before becoming the guest server. This rotational guest serving continues until all courts have been visited.

Extensions: Change the object carried on the racket; for example, use a Nerf ball or a tennis ball. Increase the distance from the net to the delivery, and have the student serve the object from farther away.

Inclusion Suggestion: Create two guest servers by positioning a student without a disability on a scooter and having that student perform in the same manner as the student with a disability.

Games-by-Skill-Level Index: Moderate- to High-Functioning Students

The index in table 6.5 is designed to address those students with disabilities who are considered to have moderate to high function. The progression for game activity is still considered the same, but a combination of skills is necessary to address skill development. You will notice in this section that several of the activities are used for the same strokes (forehand, backhand, and serve). These strokes will be combined in the activity to help develop wheelchair mobility skills simultaneously with tennis striking skills.

Table 6.5	Games-by-Skill-Level Index for Moderate- to High-Functioning Students—Wheelchair Tennis		
Skills	**Individual activity**	**Small group activity**	**Teamwork**
Forehand	Wall to Net	Reverse and Go	Mixed Doubles Plus 1
Backhand	Wall to Net	Reverse and Go	Mixed Doubles Plus 1
Serve	Wall to Net	Serving the Reverse and Go	The Serving Chair

Game Descriptions

There are a total of five activities in this section. Several of the activities are repeated for different skills. Use these activities in any combination of skill progression that meets your needs.

Skill Forehand, Backhand, Serve

◆ Wall to Net

Game Level: Individual

Formation: Individual with peer assistant

Equipment: Wall, tennis court, tennis racket, tennis balls

Description: In this activity, students with and without disabilities can practice individually on the forehand, backhand, and serve by rebounding the ball off a gymnasium wall or outside wall. Students should work for control and successive contacts before moving to another stroke (for instance, 10 forehands, then 10 backhands, and so on). Once they have success with rebounding off the wall, they may move to the court and practice hitting over a net. Students can return these strokes based on their individual skill levels. Students may have more success if those on one court practice while those on the receiving court catch and gather the balls instead of trying to return. Once one set of students has practiced, they rotate and the other set of students on the opposite side of the net hit.

Extension: For the student with a disability, make sure to adjust the type of ball to be used and the distance to the net as needed.

Inclusion Suggestions: Make sure to rotate the peer assistant throughout the class time. Students without disabilities can perform the skills from the folding chairs next to the student with a disability.

Skill Forehand and Backhand

◆ Reverse and Go

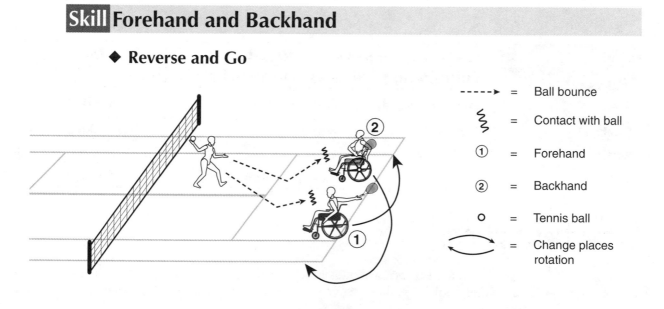

- - - ▶	=	Ball bounce
⌇	=	Contact with ball
①	=	Forehand
②	=	Backhand
○	=	Tennis ball
⌒	=	Change places rotation

Game Level: Small group

Formation: Small groups of three or four students in triangle formation

Equipment: Tennis court, tennis racket, tennis balls, traffic cones

Description: This activity can be repeated for both strokes (forehand and backhand). Divide the class into small groups and position them on the tennis court or any open space. Students should be in a triangle formation, with one student acting as the feeder and remaining students positioned to hit a forehand or backhand stroke from six feet in front of the baseline. The feeder stands about five feet from the net facing their classmates and bounces a ball to them to be struck. The student in the forehand position should use a forehand stroke and the student in the backhand position should use a backhand stroke. The bounce must be controlled and at a tempo that allows the student striking the ball to move into position to complete the stroke. Once the student using the forehand has completed their turn, they should reverse their position and travel to the backhand position. The same is true for the student who has used a backhand stroke. Once each student has completed five strokes of each type, a new student feeder should be established and the activity continued. This is not meant to be a fast-paced activity. The students should have ample time to reposition on the court to complete each new stroke. This is an excellent activity for working on wheelchair mobility skills, as it requires the student using a wheelchair to strike the ball from the side of the court, push their wheelchair to the other side, and get ready to perform a new stroke.

Extension: The student with a disability should be able to perform this activity with minimal modifications. Allow the student using the wheelchair to adjust the distance for striking the ball, and don't forget to allow two bounces from the feeder.

Inclusion Suggestion: Set up one court that has one folding chair each at the forehand and backhand positions. Students without disabilities can sit in the folding chairs to strike the tennis ball while the student with a disability acts as the feeder.

Skill Serve

◆ Serving the Reverse and Go

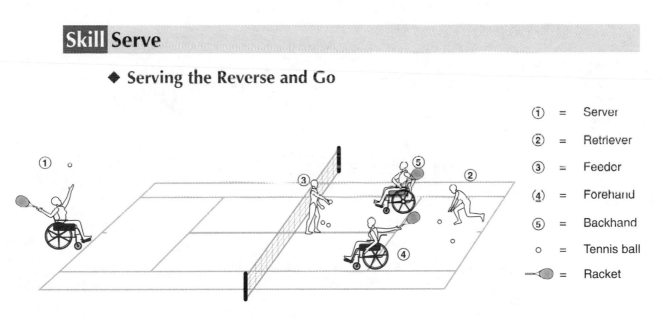

①	=	Server
②	=	Retriever
③	=	Feeder
④	=	Forehand
⑤	=	Backhand
○	=	Tennis ball
━◖	=	Racket

Game Level: Small group

Formation: Small groups of three or four students

Equipment: Tennis court, tennis racket, tennis balls, traffic cones

Description: This is the same activity as described in the game Reverse and Go, except that the activity is initiated with a serve from the opposite court. From behind the baseline on the opposite court, a student with or without a disability serves the ball to a student retriever. Once the student retriever has the ball, they must toss it to the student feeder, and the activity continues as described earlier. Make sure to rotate students through all positions.

Extension: The student with a disability should be able to perform this activity with minimal modifications. The student using the wheelchair can adjust the distance for striking the ball.

Inclusion Suggestions: Students without disabilities can sit in the folding chairs to serve the tennis ball. The student with a disability can decide which positions their teammates should take to start the activity.

Skill Forehand and Backhand

◆ Mixed Doubles Plus 1

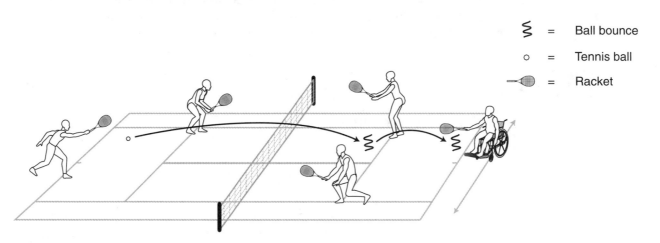

⟨	=	Ball bounce
o	=	Tennis ball
⊶	=	Racket

Game Level: Teamwork

Formation: Normal doubles formation for a tennis match, with an additional player (student with a disability) added to one team (three players on one side and two on the other)

Equipment: Tennis court, tennis racket, tennis balls or slightly deflated four-inch playground balls

Description: The activity is played the same as any doubles play, except that a student with a disability is positioned at or near the baseline for one team and responsible for all balls hit deep on the court. The student with a disability is allowed two bounces to return a ball and must attempt to use either the forehand or backhand stroke during the game. The remaining two teammates should play forward in the regular doubles position and *must return a ball before it strikes the ground.* The student using the wheelchair needs to cover the court from sideline to sideline during each rally. (This will be a very challenging game and should be reserved for your most talented students.)

Extensions: Increase the number of allowed bounces as needed for your student with a disability. Change the distance or coverage area as needed for the student using the wheelchair. Rotate the student with a disability to other teams throughout the tennis unit. Change the type of ball used in this game; a slightly deflated four-inch playground ball works well.

Inclusion Suggestion: The student with a disability can announce the score prior to any service, dependent on communication methods, such as a word board, hand gestures, or flip cards.

Skill Serve

◆ The Serving Chair

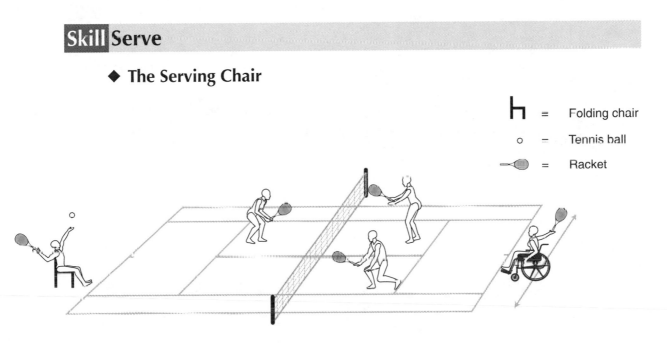

h = Folding chair

o = Tennis ball

= Racket

Game Level: Teamwork

Formation: Normal doubles formation for a tennis match, except that an additional player (student with a disability) is added to one team (three players on one side and two on the other).

Equipment: Folding chair, tennis court, tennis racket, tennis balls or slightly deflated four-inch playground ball

Description: This is the same activity as described in Mixed Doubles Plus 1, with the following exception: the team without a student with a disability must start the game serving from a seated position in a folding chair. Once the serve has been made, the folding chair is removed, and play continues as described earlier.

Extensions: Place a folding chair on each court, and require all students to serve from a seated position. Change the size and weight of the ball; a slightly deflated four-inch playground ball often works well.

Inclusion Suggestion: The student with a disability can assign classmates to the various teams.

PART IV

COURT GAMES/ TRACK EVENTS

Chapter 7   Goalball

Chapter 8   The Slalom

chapter

7

Goalball

Goalball is a sport played by individuals who are blind or visually impaired. The game is played indoors on a court the size of a volleyball court. The sport of goalball is governed by the United States Association of Blind Athletes (USABA), which was founded in 1976. More than 3,000 athletes are represented by the USABA across several sports, including alpine and nordic skiing, judo, powerlifting, swimming, tandem cycling, track and field, and wrestling. Individuals who are members of the USABA can also participate in international competition for some of these sports and are represented by the International Blind Sports Association, or IBSA.

Description of the Sport

In goalball two teams, consisting of three members each, oppose each other at opposite ends of the court. All players wear eye shades. The game is played by trying to roll (referred to as a "throw") the goalball past the opposition's goal line, which is the back line of the court. The goalball emits an auditory cue, made by bells within the ball, to help the players track the path of the thrown ball. Each player has a specific area to cover according to their position as they try to stop the rolled ball. Players must attempt to stop the rolled ball and, if successful, quickly return it toward the opposition in hopes of throwing it past them for a score. Players hold a stationary position during play, moving only to slide and block the ball.

Field of Play

The goalball court is 60 feet long and 30 feet wide and is divided into three areas that extend the width of the court. The middle of the court is called the neutral area and is 20 feet long. The remaining two areas are called the throwing area and team area; they are marked for each team and are 10 feet long.

To help the players recognize their areas of play, narrow rope or clothesline is placed on the floor and covered by floor tape to create a tactile border around each section of the court. Lines marking team areas are parallel to and 10 feet from the back or goal lines. High ball lines, which start the neutral area and are explained later, are marked parallel to and 20 feet from the back or goal lines. The center line is marked parallel to and midway between the two goal lines. In addition, small pieces of rope are covered with tape to help mark the player positions of center, left wing, and right wing.

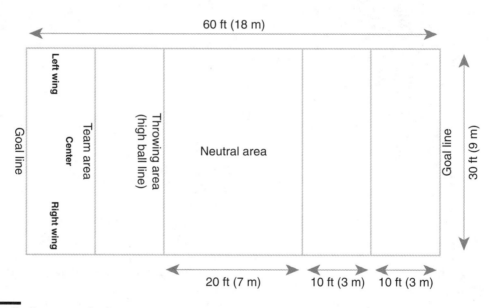

Goalball court with player positions.

Players

Individuals who are blind or have a visual impairment can play goalball. The degree of vision is not an issue with goalball since all players must wear eye shades. Official USABA players must adhere to the following sport classifications of visual impairment:

- A person classified as B1 has vision ranges from no light perception in either eye up to and including the ability to perceive light. There is no visual ability to recognize objects in any direction or at any distance.
- A person classified as B2 can see at two meters what a person with normal vision can see at 60 meters (i.e., below 2/60 vision) and/or has a field of vision less than five degrees.

- A person classified as B3 can recognize objects between two and six meters away. They can see what a person with normal vision can see at 60 meters (i.e., 2/60 to 6/60 vision) and/or have a field of vision between 5 and 20 degrees.

You might choose to use another form of classification not specific to sport. It is referred to as a classification of blindness and is sometimes used by school districts to identify students' disabilities.

- Legally blind: 20/200 vision, or seeing at 20 feet what someone with normal vision sees at 200 feet.

- Travel vision: 5/200 to 10/200 vision, or seeing at 5 to10 feet what someone with normal vision sees at 200 feet.

- Motion vision: 3/200 to 5/200 vision, or seeing at 3 to 5 feet what someone with normal vision sees at 200 feet.

- Light perception: Less than 3/200 vision, or the ability to distinguish a strong light at a distance of three feet from the eye. A person with this classification cannot detect hand motion three feet from the eye.

- Total blindness: The inability to recognize light shone directly into the eye.

Equipment

The official goals, which resemble soccer goal nets, are 30 feet wide and 4 feet high and are positioned on the goal line. If you decide to construct your own goals with PVC pipe or lumber, make sure that the corners and edges are padded. Goals are not needed to play the game in your physical education classes.

The ball is approximately the size of a basketball and is made of very durable rubber. Inside the ball are a set of bells, similar to jingle bells, that roll freely when the ball is rolled from one end of the court to the other. The sound of the bells helps the player track the location of the ball. For information about purchasing a goalball, contact the USABA. (See appendix D.)

Eye shades must be worn by all players any time they are on the court. During official competition, players are not allowed to touch or adjust their eye shades while on the court. If eye shade adjustment is needed, players must ask the referee for permission to do so.

Hip, elbow, and knee padding is recommended for all players since the method of blocking a thrown ball is to execute a dive-and-block movement. Players must be taught how to position their bodies in preparation for such a move to avoid injury. Since blocking is an aggressive movement, only players with appropriate padding will be able to block with minimal risk of injury. You might be able to secure hip pads from your school's football program and elbow and knee pads from the wrestling team. You might also be able to construct your own padding using foam padding and elastic athletic bandages.

Starting the Game

A coin toss decides which team will be awarded the ball and which team will defend a chosen goal. All players on the court must wear eye shades and should be familiar with their location on the court. A brief period of court orientation is allowed prior to the start of an official game.

Game Objective

The objective of the game is to throw the goalball past the opponents' back line or end line into the goal net. There are three player positions on the court, a center and two wings. The center position must cover from sideline to sideline within the team area and stands about two to three feet in front of the wings. The two wings must cover a smaller area, usually one body length from the sideline to their playing position. Player movement is limited. All players start in a standing position commonly referred to as a basic athletic stance. When the ball is thrown, the players must be able to move quickly to block the ball by dropping down and sliding to the side of the sound made by the oncoming ball.

Basic player positions for throwing.

Blocking a goalball is made from a horizontal position on the floor. If a player blocks a thrown ball, they must be able to rise to their feet as quickly as possible to return the ball. Once the player has secured a block, the ball must be returned to the opponents' end of the court within eight seconds. Since no player is allowed to throw a ball more than two consecutive times, passing is very important.

Basic player positions for blocking.

Passing among teammates is allowed and should be practiced. If a ball is blocked by the right winger, that teammate may pass it to the left winger or center player for a return throw. Passes are made by rolling the ball across the floor to a teammate quietly enough so as not to tip off the new position of the goalball to the opponents. Passing becomes a very strategic offensive maneuver as one team tries to attack the other's court by throwing the ball at the opponent's end of the court.

Game Length

The USABA has established an official game length of two 7-minute halves, or 14 total minutes. In the case of an overtime, the teams will play two additional three-minute halves. A second coin toss is used to determine which team will throw first in the overtime.

General Rules/Penalties

Because the sport of goalball does not have a corresponding sport for individuals without disabilities, the rules discussed in this chapter will be specific to the sport.

Rules Specific to Goalball

Coaches or teachers may escort any starting player or substitute to their playing position. Once the game has begun, however, players are responsible for maintaining their playing positions throughout the game. Players should use the tactile lines on the court to help with court orientation.

The ball must be rolling as it crosses the offensive team's throwing line and enters the neutral area. The ball cannot be airborne. If the ball is airborne, it will be ruled a "high ball" and awarded to the opponent team.

If the ball rolls to a stop in the neutral area and no player makes an attempt to control the ball, it is considered a "dead ball." Dead ball rulings are awarded to the defending team at the time of play. If a ball rebounds off a player from a block and rolls to a stop in the neutral area, the ball will be returned to the throwing team. This same rule applies should a ball rebound off a goalpost and roll dead into the neutral area.

If a player throws a ball in such a manner as to not have floor contact in the neutral area, it is considered a "long ball" and the throw is nullified. The ball is then turned over to the defending team.

During play, if a player attempts to pass to a teammate and the pass goes out of bounds, the play is considered an infraction. All infractions result in turnovers to the defending team.

The two types of penalties enforced in goalball are personal and team penalties. When a penalty is enforced, a penalty shot is awarded. During a penalty shot, all players from the penalized team must clear the floor with the exception of one player. The ball is awarded to the nonpenalized team for a penalty shot. The penalized team can only defend the goal with one player. The player that remains to defend against the penalty shot is determined by the type of penalty committed. In the case of a personal penalty, the player committing the penalty must defend the goal single-handedly. In the case of a team penalty, the last player to throw from the penalized team must defend the goal single-handedly. Once the penalty shot is completed, play is stopped and the penalized team is allowed to return to the court.

The following are examples of personal penalties:

- Illegal touch of the eye shades while on the court. No player is allowed to use vision to detect the thrown ball. Once the players are on the court, they are not allowed to adjust their eye shades or blindfolds. Feel free to modify this rule based on your teaching situation.

- Throwing the ball for a third consecutive time. Remember, no player is allowed to throw more than two consecutive times.

- Some form of illegal defense. Players must remain at their playing positions when defending and must remain in the team area of the court.

- Unfair play. Players must remain relatively quiet during competition. Any loud, inappropriate verbal calls from players to their teammates on the bench could be considered unfair play.

The following are examples of team penalties:

- Eight-second delay. Teams have only eight seconds to return a throw once they have gained possession.
- Team delay. Teams not prepared to start play on time or player substitutions being made without notifying the referee are considered team delays.
- Unfair play. Similar to the ruling of unfair play mentioned for personal penalties.

Summary of the Sport

Table 7.1 includes the basic information you will need to conduct a goalball game. Use this table as a quick reference in your physical education classes.

Table 7.1	Overview of Goalball
Field of play	Volleyball court: 60 ft by 30 ft Goal width: 30 ft center on the back line; goal height: 4 ft Team area and throwing area: 30 ft by 10 ft; neutral area: 30 ft by 20 ft
Players	Maximum allowed on court is three per team
Equipment	Goalball (specially made; contact USABA national office in Colorado Springs, CO). Goals (to include netting) are not needed for teaching in physical education class. Eye shades or blindfolds, knee pads, elbow pads, hip pads
Legal start	The game is started with a toss of a coin. The winner can choose to throw first or defend a favored goal.
Ball movement	A player may use only their hands to move the ball; no kicking is allowed. A player may only throw two consecutive times when attacking. Passing is allowed within team area; however, once the team has established control of the ball, they have 8 sec to return a throw. Balls passed out of bounds are awarded to the opponents.
Infractions	All infractions result in turnovers to the defending team. **Examples:** • Long ball throw: A thrown ball not touching the neutral area • Premature throw: Throwing the ball before allowed to by the referee • Stepover: The whole foot stepping out of bounds during a throw • Passout: Passing the ball out of bounds to a teammate • Ball-over: Balls blocked into the neutral area and considered "dead" are awarded to the throwing team.
Penalties	All penalties are in two categories (personal or team) and result in a penalty shot. **Personal penalties:** • High ball: An offensive throw that does not touch in the neutral area • Eye shades: A player touching or adjusting their eye shades while on the court • Third time throw: Throwing a ball more than two consecutive times • Illegal defense: Defensive contact by a player outside of the team area • Unfair play: Ruled by the referee as behaving inappropriately

Team penalties:
- Eight seconds: Taking longer than 8 sec to return a thrown ball
- Team delay of game: Team not ready to play at the start; any actions to prevent play
- Unfair team play: Similar to personal unfair play
- Illegal coaching: Coaching from bench area during the competition; coaching from the bench is allowed during time-outs.

Skills to Be Taught

Three basic skills will be addressed for goalball: throwing, blocking, and passing. These three skills should be adequate to help you teach students with visual impairments or who are blind. Students who are not visually impaired or blind will enjoy the athleticism involved in the sport. Goalball is a team game that requires players to work together during offensive and defensive phases of the game.

Although the skill is called throwing, the execution is generally considered a one-handed roll of the ball across the court to the opponents' goal area. The goalball should be thrown rapidly and with enough force to carry it the length of the court. The speed and accuracy of the throw will be determined by the skill level of your students. You have the option of adjusting court dimensions to better suit your students' levels of performance. You also can start new players with a two-handed throw.

Blocking a thrown ball is the heart of the defense. A student must listen closely for the sound of the ball rolling toward them and move quickly to block as the ball nears their location. To execute the block, the student must dive to the floor and lie on their side facing the oncoming ball. In the block position the student should have their arms and legs extended, attempting to make their bodies as long as possible. Each student should work to keep the legs together so that the ball does not pass through the legs while on the floor. As both arms are extended overhead, the top arm should be dropped low enough to cover and protect the student's face. Once the ball is blocked, the student must gain control of the ball for a return throw or pass it to a teammate.

Throwing

This explanation will be for a right-handed student using a one-handed delivery and a simple three-step approach. The stance and approach to throwing a goalball is similar to that of delivering a bowling ball. To execute the throw, the student takes a left, right, left step approach. The first step (left) should be short and quick, followed by a second (right) and third (left) step with longer strides. During the first step, the student swings the goalball back while supporting it from underneath with the right hand. On the second step, the student brings the goalball forward with force as the body is lowered close to the floor. On the third step, the student slides on the left foot with the body in a low release position. The ball is released on the slide forward as the student plants the left foot, lifting the throwing hand for follow-through.

Basic throwing stance.

Swing the goalball back during the approach for throwing.

Low body position upon release and follow-through.

Blocking

Students start in a basic "athletic" position, which means the feet are shoulder-width apart, body weight is evenly distributed on both feet, knees are slightly flexed, arms are held forward, hands are about at waist height, and elbows are slightly flexed. For a ball approaching from the right, the student takes a short jab step to the right and begins to lower the body into the path of the oncoming ball. The student continues facing the ball as it approaches and must avoid turning their back to the ball. As the ball nears the body, the student makes initial contact with the floor with hands and arms to cushion floor contact. Once the hands and arms are in contact with the floor, the student quickly lowers the knees and hips on the right side of the body. As the entire body reaches the floor, the student strives to make themselves as long as possible, keeping the arms stretched out over the head and protecting the face with the top arm. The final blocking position is lying on the right side with arms extended, legs together, and the left arm across the face. This same technique works for a ball approaching from the left. To block a ball approaching head-on, the student eliminates the first jab step and simply tries to assume the blocking position as quickly as possible. Most students will attempt to block

Basic athletic position in preparation to block.

Short step to the side of a block.

Hands, elbows, and knees contact the floor early.

Side-lying position, arms extended, legs together, face protected during block.

goalballs thrown directly at them by just dropping directly to the floor on their dominant side.

Passing

Passing is accomplished by rolling the ball from teammate to teammate in a more controlled fashion, with the ball traveling less than six meters. Passes can be executed with one or two hands. The key to passing is to move the ball in such a manner as to have a teammate, and not an opponent, hear the ball. To accomplish this, the student faces a teammate and lifts the ball from the floor about four to five inches. With the ball held slightly off the floor, the student swings and releases it toward a teammate so that it drops to the floor loudly enough to rattle the bells inside the ball. If the ball is not lifted and dropped to initiate the pass, the bells inside will not make enough noise to help a teammate locate the oncoming pass.

Locating a teammate in order to execute an accurate pass must be accomplished as discretely as possible. Since it is not advantageous for teammates to use frequent verbal communication, a system of tapping on the floor is recommended to request or receive a pass. Students might establish a numbering system to help identify one another—for example, one tap is the right wing player, two taps is the left wing, and three taps is the center, or whatever combination you design.

Teams could work together to execute two passes (for example, right wing to left wing, left wing to center, ending with a center return throw) before returning a throw at the opponent. Keep in mind that such a maneuver needs to take place within the eight-second limit.

Face teammate and lift the ball in preparation to pass.

Locate a teammate to execute an accurate pass.

Functional Profiles and General Modifications

The functional profiles for students who are blind or have a visual impairment are not related to their disability, but rather to their ability. The sport of goalball requires all players to wear eye shades or a blindfold, thus equalizing the disability. As a result, a player classified as having minimal vision is equal to a player who has no vision. The difference in the players' performance is related more to their ambulatory skills and level of independent movement.

To play the sport of goalball, the student must be able to hold the ball, throw the ball, and block the ball independently. These skills require the student to have sufficient levels of physical fitness and motor coordination to move laterally, drop to the floor, and rise to their feet without assistance. Functional profiles for this sport will focus on levels of assistance needed by the student and not on levels of visual acuity or field of vision.

Table 7.2 suggests student profiles that might fit your teaching situation. After determining your students' levels of ability, consider the activity modifications listed in table 7.3.

Table 7.2	Student Functional Profiles for Goalball
Functional skill level	**Student profile**
Low	Unable to hold a goalball, move to locate a thrown ball, lower body to floor, or rise to stand from blocking position independently
Moderate	Able to hold a goalball independently with two hands; has moderate physical fitness level; able to lower body to floor and assume blocking position, but needs minimal assistance to rise from blocking position
High	Able to hold a goalball with one or two hands, lower body to floor and assume proper blocking position, and rise to stand from blocking position independently

General Modifications

Table 7.3 suggests general modifications to the three skills necessary to play goalball. Notice that these modifications are suggested according to student functional profiles. You can decide how to apply these general modifications to your specific student population.

Table 7.3	General Modifications for Goalball	
Skill level	**Skill**	**Activity modifications**
Low	Throwing	Use lighter ball that is tethered for support. Practice pushing the ball to simulate the throwing action.
	Blocking	Block a thrown ball from a kneeling position while supported from behind.
	Passing	Push a heavier ball (medicine ball) on a tabletop while seated.
Moderate	Throwing	Receive assistance with hand-over-hand technique while attempting a one-handed throw.
	Blocking	Block from a kneeling position. Use a folding chair to assist movement from kneeling to standing after blocking.
	Passing	No modifications: Execute pass with current level of two-handed throw.
High	All skills	No modifications: Used with highest-functioning students.

Game Progressions

The games listed in the remainder of this chapter are presented in the same sequence as in previous chapters (individual, to small group, to teamwork). Keep in mind that you are trying to support inclusion in all three learning domains (psychomotor, cognitive, and affective).

Games-by-Skill-Level Index: Low-Functioning Students

The index in table 7.4 will help you choose games according to the skill you want to teach and the ability level of your student with a visual impairment. This first index is for low-functioning students who require a high degree of assistance. Very low-functioning students will need to begin with individual games and may progress into small group and teamwork situations as their skills improve. Some students may be able to begin in a small group or even a teamwork situation. The decision is yours to make (with some help from the student, if appropriate). The index is followed by descriptions of the games listed.

Table 7.4	Games-by-Skill-Level Index for Low-Functioning Students—Goalball		
Skills	**Individual activity**	**Small group activity**	**Teamwork**
Throwing	Up It Goes	Throw It Out I	Throw It Out II
Blocking	Don't Go There I	Don't Go There II	Don't Go There III
Passing	Here I am	Remember Me I	Zigzag Relay

Game Descriptions

Each game description in this section includes game level, formation, equipment, description, extensions, and inclusion suggestions. You may select any game that you feel matches the ability level of your students who have a visual impairment. Again, these games are written with the idea of moving a student from an individual situation to a teamwork environment.

Skill Throwing

◆ Up It Goes

Game Level: Individual

Formation: Individual with peer assistant

Equipment: Basketball, medicine ball, or goalball

Description: The student with a visual impairment is seated on the floor with the ball positioned between the legs. The student lifts the ball with two hands and holds it up for a count of 10 seconds.

Extensions: Increase the time of the lift by five-second increments. A teacher's aide or student from the class can sit behind the student and use a hand-over-hand technique to assist with the lift. The student can also change from a seated position to a kneeling position every three lifts.

Inclusion Suggestion: Witnessed by the teacher, the student can verbalize to two friends in class their accomplishment.

◆ Throw It Out I

Game Level: Small group

Formation: Students with and without disabilities wear blindfolds and sit in a circle formation on the floor.

Equipment: Basketball, medicine ball, or goalball; blindfolds or eye shades

Description: Students throw the ball (roll it) around the circle while seated using two hands as needed. On a signal from the teacher, the student with the ball tries to throw the ball out of the circle. Students must become familiar with the position of everyone in their circle as they must try to throw the ball out. Likewise, students can be working on early blocking skills by listening carefully to the roll of the ball and attempting to block the ball from exiting the circle.

Extensions: Play one game from a seated position, then move to a kneeling position. Increase the size of the circle as the students' skill levels improve.

Inclusion Suggestion: Rotate new students without visual impairments into the circle, and have the student with a visual impairment explain the rules of the game.

◆ Throw It Out II

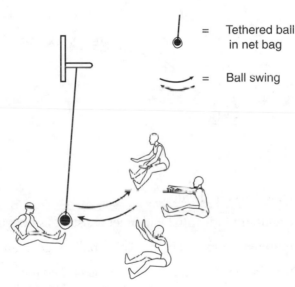

Game Level: Teamwork

Formation: Three sighted students sit in a semicircle around a student with a visual impairment.

Equipment: Basketball, goalball, or medicine ball; net for hanging the ball from a basketball rim

Description: The ball hangs all the way to the floor from the basketball rim. The student holding the tethered ball is in the starting position previously described for throwing. You will need to provide hand-over-hand assistance, placing your hand over the student's hands as they initiate movement, to help balance the ball. Three sighted teammates are in front of this student in a semicircle formation. The student with a visual impairment steps and throws the ball according to the skill sequence described for throwing to each teammate. The student is working on step sequence, release, and follow-through. Since the ball is tethered, it will swing out and will not be rolling on the floor; the student should be ready to catch the ball on the return swing from each teammate. The objective is to work around the semicircle throwing to all teammates, who are using an auditory cue (floor tapping) to request the throw.

Extension: Widen the distance between the students in the semicircle.

Inclusion Suggestion: The student with a visual impairment can demonstrate the activity to the entire class.

Skill Blocking

◆ Don't Go There I

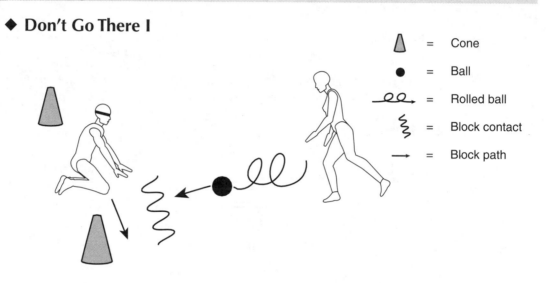

△	=	Cone
●	=	Ball
⌇⌇→	=	Rolled ball
⌇	=	Block contact
→	=	Block path

Game Level: Individual

Formation: Individual with peer assistant as needed

Equipment: Basketball, medicine ball, or goalball; traffic cones

Description: The student with a visual impairment kneels between two cones placed three feet apart. A sighted partner attempts to roll the ball past the student and between the cones. The objective for the student with a visual impairment is to block the ball from passing between the cones. Use a partial hand-over-hand technique to assist the student with blocking.

Extensions: Increase the distance between the cones, or increase the distance between the student and ball release.

Inclusion Suggestion: The student with a visual impairment can determine the distances for throwing once their skill level has improved.

◆ Don't Go There II

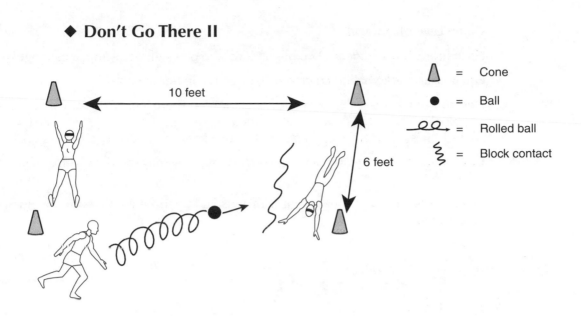

Game Level: Small group

Formation: Three students, two blindfolded and one without a blindfold, positioned within a small 10-foot-by-6-foot area

Equipment: Basketball, medicine ball, or goalball; traffic cones

Description: Create a small working rectangular area (e.g., 10 feet by 6 feet) using traffic cones. A blindfolded student is at each end of the area, lying down between the cones. The objective is to block a thrown ball while lying on the floor at each end. The sighted student alternates throws, keeping track of how many blocks were made.

Extensions: Increase the distance of the rectangle or rotate the students.

Inclusion Suggestion: The student with a visual impairment can decide which end should block first.

◆ Don't Go There III

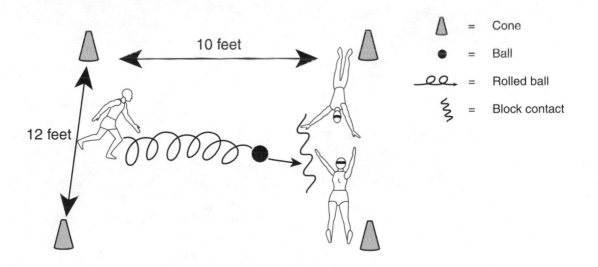

Game Level: Teamwork

Formation: Three students, two blindfolded and one sighted, within a rectangular area

Equipment: Basketball, medicine ball, or goalball; traffic cones

Description: Increase the rectangle from Don't Go There II to a 10-foot-by-12-foot area. The blockers are at the *same end* of the rectangle across the opening between the cones. As the ball is rolled at the opening, the two blockers must work together to stop the ball.

Extension: Once students have blocked the ball, they may stand up with the ball; assist as needed.

Inclusion Suggestion: The student with a visual impairment can report the number of blocks made.

Skill Passing

◆ Here I Am

Game Level: Individual

Formation: Individual with peer assistant as needed

Equipment: Basketball, medicine ball, or goalball; traffic cones

Description: Seated or standing, the student with a visual impairment holds the ball (provide assistance as needed). A sighted student approximately six feet away taps on the floor until the student with a visual impairment passes the ball correctly.

Extension: The student without a visual impairment can change locations after each successful pass; work for three consecutive successful passes before changing locations.

Inclusion Suggestion: The student with a visual impairment can decide how many successful passes should be made before the sighted student changes locations.

◆ Remember Me I

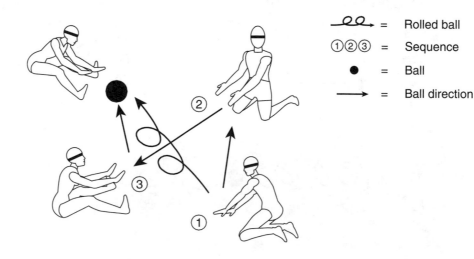

~~ℓℓ~~→ =	Rolled ball
①②③ =	Sequence
● =	Ball
⟶ =	Ball direction

Game Level: Small group

Formation: Students with and without visual impairments are wearing blindfolds and sitting in a small circle on the floor.

Equipment: Basketball, medicine ball, or goalball; traffic cones; blindfolds

Description: On a signal the students pass the goalball back and forth across the circle. The objective of the activity is to pass the ball around the circle in the same sequence as the original pattern, meaning that once the ball has been passed around the circle and everyone has touched it, the second time around should follow the same pattern, with students passing to the same individual each trip. Each pass is preceded by a tapping on the floor by the receiver.

Extension: Work for minimizing physical assistance for the student with a visual impairment. Have the group alternate positions: first seated, then kneeling, then standing. Vary the diameter of the circle with each round.

Inclusion Suggestion: The student with a visual impairment can determine the sequence of passing positions (for example, seated-kneeling-standing or kneeling-seated-standing).

◆ Zigzag Relay

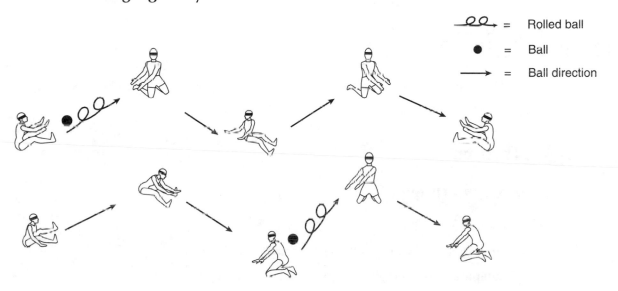

Game Level: Teamwork

Formation: Students are seated on the floor in two lines ready for a passing relay. Stagger teammates about six feet apart so that the pattern of passing the ball will be zigzag.

Equipment: Basketball, medicine ball, or goalball; blindfolds

Description: All students wear blindfolds. On a signal the ball is passed to the next person, who is using a tapping signal to receive the pass. Continue passing the ball to the opposite end. The first team who passes the ball to the opposite end wins.

Extension: Students can move from a seated position, to kneeling, and then to standing.

Inclusion Suggestion: The student with a visual impairment can determine in what order their teammates are positioned and be allowed to change those positions with each race.

Games-by-Skill-Level Index: Moderate- to High-Functioning Students

The index in table 7.5 is designed to help you choose games for your students with visual impairments or who are blind, with moderate to high skill levels. The progression of activity suggestions remains the same: from individual, to small group, to teamwork.

Table 7.5	Games-by-Skill-Level Index for Moderate- to High-Functioning Students—Goalball		
Skills	**Individual activity**	**Small group activity**	**Teamwork**
Throwing	Step to Throw I	Step to Throw II	Step to Throw III
Blocking	Slide Over	Block It	Four Square
Passing	Here I am	Remember Me II	Work It Across

Game Descriptions

The following games are suggested for students you consider to be more mobile. As always, feel free to modify them as needed.

Skill Throwing

◆ Step to Throw I

Game Level: Individual

Formation: Individual with peer assistant as needed

Equipment: Basketball, medicine ball, or goalball; traffic cones

Description: This activity will require the student to concentrate on footwork while throwing. Using the teaching points from the skill description presented earlier in this chapter, have the student hold the goalball with one hand and work on taking a one-step slide delivery as they release the ball to a sighted partner about 10 feet away. The sighted partner should make some type of auditory noise (whistle, floor tap) to give the student a reference for throwing.

Extensions: Move the sighted partner to various locations within the 10-foot radius. Have the sighted partner roll the ball back, and have the student with a visual impairment work on blocking the return throw from a kneeling position. Rotate the sighted partners from the members of the class. Have the sighted partners wear blindfolds after several rotations through the activity.

Inclusion Suggestion: The student with a visual impairment can call out the location of the sighted partner before throwing using the partner's name (for example, "Tom, you are on the right side"). Once the student has identified where the partner is standing, they can redirect their partner to establish a new target location.

◆ Step to Throw II

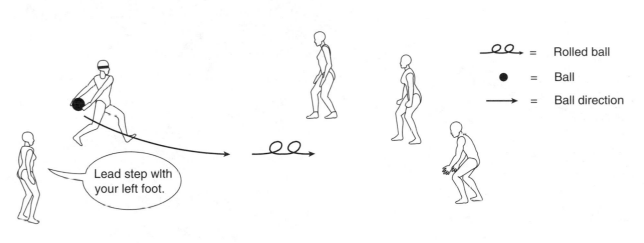

Lead step with your left foot.

⟋⟍QQ →	=	Rolled ball
●	=	Ball
⟶	=	Ball direction

Game Level: Small group

Formation: The same basic formation as Step to Throw I, except that there are three target partners and one partner assistant

Equipment: Basketball, medicine ball, or goalball; traffic cones

Description: The student with a visual impairment works on the one-handed throw, this time incorporating a three-step approach. The student assistant stands next to the student throwing and verbalizes the appropriate cues as the student throws—or example, "Ready, lead step with your left foot, quick step with your right foot, bring the ball back, now slide forward on your left foot, plant your foot, and release." The three target partners provide feedback as to the success of the throw—for instance, "Great throw, Sally, that was right at me." The distance should be at least 10 meters, or approximately 30 feet.

Extension: Add an orientation line for the student to find before each throw. For example, cut a small piece of cord, cover it with floor tape to a spot on the floor, and have the student throw from the line each time. To help with orientation, have the student locate the line each time after throwing by bending over and feeling for the line. This line will simulate their orientation line on the official court.

Inclusion Suggestion: The student with a visual impairment can determine the sequence of throws.

◆ Step to Throw III

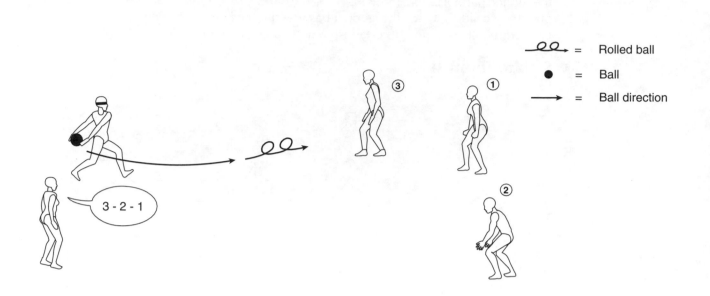

Game Level: Teamwork

Formation: The same basic formation as Step to Throw II

Equipment: Basketball, medicine ball, or goalball; traffic cones

Description: Each target partner has a number: 1, 2, 3, and so on. The student with a visual impairment throws three balls in succession according to the sequence of numbers provided by the partner assistant. For example, if the partner assistant says, "3-1-2," that means the student must throw the ball first to the student worth three points, then to the student worth one point, and finally to the student worth two points. Target partners should provide verbal feedback related to the success of the throw.

Extension: Play a math game with the student throwing (for example, "Throw the ball to the student whose number represents three minus two"). Create two teams and have a math challenge.

Inclusion Suggestion: The student with a visual impairment can determine the math challenge (for example, "What are two numbers that add up to five?").

Skill Blocking

◆ Slide Over

△	= Cone
●	= Ball
→	= Block path
ℓℓ→	= Rolled ball
ξ	= Contact block

Game Level: Individual

Formation: Individual with peer assistant as needed

Equipment: Basketball, medicine ball, or goalball; traffic cones; blindfolds

Description: The student who is blocking starts in a kneeling position. A sighted partner stands about six feet in front of the student with a visual impairment. The student with a visual impairment must wear a blindfold. The sighted partner rolls three balls to the left and three to the right, allowing enough time between each throw for the student with a visual impairment to return to their starting position. The objective is to have the student with a visual impairment block the rolled balls.

Extension: Move the student from a kneeling position to a standing position.

Inclusion Suggestion: The student who is blocking can demonstrate to the class, then verbalize all the points they have to remember to block a rolled ball (for example, "I have to listen carefully for the ball. Then I have to move quickly to the right or left and lead with my hands and arms. Then I have to dive to the floor and make my body long to block").

◆ Block It

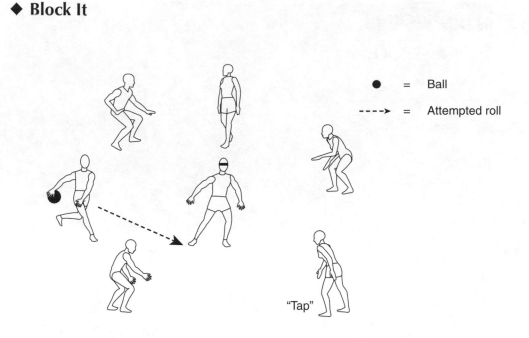

● = Ball

-----> = Attempted roll

"Tap"

Game Level: Small group

Formation: Six students in a circle formation (15 feet in diameter) and a student with a visual impairment in the center wearing a blindfold

Equipment: Basketball, medicine ball, or goalball; traffic cones; blindfolds

Description: The objective of the game is to get the ball across the circle without having it blocked by the student in the middle. If the ball is blocked three times, a new student plays the middle position, and the student with a visual impairment joins the others in the circle. The student in the middle should start in the basic athletic position. The students in the circle should tap the ball to the floor one time prior to throwing it across the circle to provide some type of auditory cue for the blocker.

Extensions: Change the number of times a ball should be blocked—once, twice, and so on. Alternate the student blocking the ball from a kneeling to a standing position.

Inclusion Suggestion: The student blocking can determine the diameter of the circle.

◆ Four Square

◯	=	Students without visual impairment
⊖	=	Students blindfolded
—	=	Taped line
⌒⌒→	=	Rolled ball
§§	=	Contact block
①②③④	=	Teams

Game Level: Teamwork

Formation: Four traffic cones mark the corners of a square about 25 feet by 25 feet. A taped orientation line, about three feet in length, is centered on each side of the square.

Equipment: Basketball, medicine ball, or goalball; traffic cones; blindfolds

Description: There are four 2-person teams (each side of the square hosts a team): one student wearing a blindfold on each of the orientation lines and one sighted person behind that student. One of the students with the blindfold should be a student. The objective of the game is to throw the goalball across the square at an opponent in an attempt to get it past the blocker. If the ball is blocked, that student should recover, find the orientation line, and return a throw. The throws may be at opposite or adjacent sides of the square. Blockers should be standing in the "up and ready" position.

Extensions: Increase the size or number of the squares. Rotate all students as blockers.

Inclusion Suggestion: The student with a visual impairment can keep score and report it at the end.

Skill Passing

◆ Here I Am

Game Level: Individual

Formation: Individual with a peer assistant as needed

Equipment: Basketball, medicine ball, or goalball; traffic cones

Description: The student with a visual impairment should be paired with a sighted partner, and both students should be standing in a ready position. The sighted student stands approximately 10 feet away, facing the student with a visual impairment. To work on passing, have the student without a visual impairment tap on the floor to indicate where they want the pass to travel. Both students work together to establish smooth, coordinated passing.

Extension: The student without a visual impairment can change locations after each successful pass; work for three consecutive successful passes before changing locations.

Inclusion Suggestion: The student with a visual impairment can decide how many successful passes should be made before the sighted student changes locations.

◆ Remember Me II

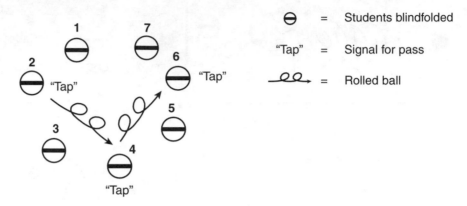

⊖ =	Students blindfolded
"Tap" =	Signal for pass
⟿ =	Rolled ball

Game Level: Small group

Formation: Students with and without visual impairments are in a small circle (approximately 25 feet in diameter) wearing blindfolds and standing in the ready position. Each student has a number.

Equipment: Basketball, medicine ball, or goalball; traffic cones; blindfolds

Description: On a signal the students pass the goalball back and forth across the circle using an "odd" or "even" call. For example, if the call is "odd," the passes only travel to the students with odd numbers and vice versa for the "even" call. To help with the passing, receivers precede each passing with a tapping on the floor.

Extension: Create math problems for the group and have them successfully complete the number of passes derived from the math problem (for example, how much is 10 plus 2?) The group should complete 12 successful passes.

Inclusion Suggestion: The student with a visual impairment can create the math problem.

◆ Work It Across

⊖	=	Students blindfolded
ℓℓ→	=	Rolled ball
⌇	=	Block
---->	=	Pass
▬	=	Taped orientation line

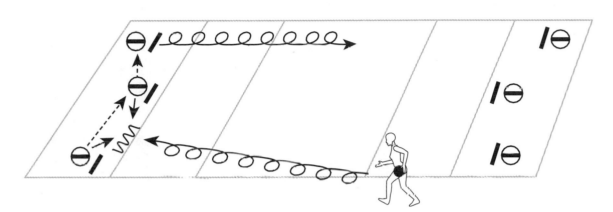

Game Level: Teamwork

Formation: Students are standing in a ready position in regulation positions on the court (i.e., center, right wing, left wing). An orientation line exists for each position.

Equipment: Basketball, medicine ball, or goalball; traffic cones; blindfolds; thin rope; floor tape

Description: Players are in their court positions and have located their orientation lines. The teacher or designated student throws a ball from the opposite end of the court to simulate an actual game. The players respond to the thrown ball by blocking it, securing it, then passing it across the court to each other. The passes must be made to all players before a return throw can be made. For example, if the opposition throw is blocked by the right winger, that player must pass it to the center, then the center must pass it to the left winger before a return throw can occur.

Extension: Increase the number of passes to be made; call out a sequence in which to make the passes (for example, right wing, left wing, center).

Inclusion Suggestion: The student with a visual impairment can determine the sequence of passing.

chapter

8

The Slalom

The slalom is a track and field event for athletes with cerebral palsy (CP) and is sanctioned by local and regional chapters of the National Disability Sports Alliance (NDSA). This event is designed for athletes that have severe physical limitations due to CP and must use a power or electric wheelchair. The slalom offers an alternative track event for individuals who are unable to sprint race in their wheelchairs. The event is part of NDSA's track competition, but it has a much broader application to other individuals with similar types of disabilities. Individuals with limiting conditions such as muscular dystrophy, spinal cord injury (quadriplegia), spina bifida, or other similar disabilities who cannot manually propel their wheelchairs can participate in this event during your physical education class. In addition, students without disabilities can be challenged by the slalom with minimal modifications such as scooter boards.

Description of the Sport

The slalom must be conducted on a hard, level surface. Although competition has been conducted indoors, traditionally it is held outdoors. Outdoor surfaces that allow sufficient room include tennis courts, the high jump area near a track, or a staging area for sprinters. Perhaps the best location is a blacktop surface near a track or gymnasium.

Students competing in the slalom must race their wheelchairs through six obstacles as fast as possible. Each obstacle presents a challenge for the student to control their wheelchair without accumulating penalty points or seconds. Each time a student makes a mistake at an obstacle, they accumulate penalty seconds, which are added to their total time.

The slalom course must be clearly marked and taped with directional arrows that indicate the proper order in which to attack the course. Students and teachers (coaches) are permitted to walk the course once prior to competition, but they are not permitted to practice the obstacles during the walk-through. During official competition, the course is closed 15 minutes prior to the event.

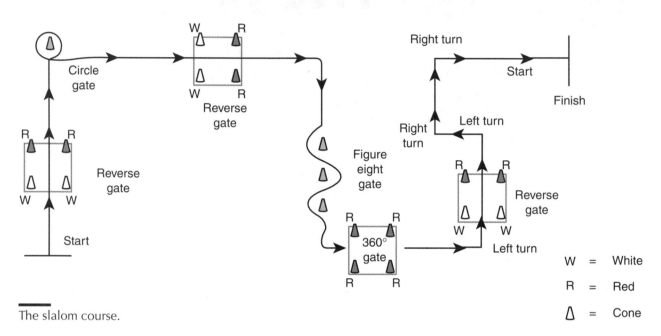

The slalom course.

Field of Play

The slalom course is set up on a hard, level surface. There should be 13 feet (four meters) between each obstacle with enough room for a straight sprint at the end of the course.

Players

Official competition is conducted for individuals who have CP or other disabling conditions that require the use of a power or electric wheelchair.

Equipment

To set up the slalom event, you will need several rolls of floor tape to mark the direction of the course and placement of the obstacles. You will also need a total of 26 markers. Official markers are cut from PVC pipe and stand 16 inches high with a four-inch diameter. You are free to use alternatives for your situation (e.g., plastic bowling pins) as long as the markers are white. You will need red ribbon or cloth, cut into short strips to tie around six markers, and white flags to place inside four of the markers. The colors of white and red have a significant meaning to the participant: each color indicates a change in the direction of travel while moving through the markers.

The markers are used to form gates that the student must maneuver through. There are three reverse gates, one 360-degree gate, a circle gate, and a figure-eight gate. Reverse and 360-degree gates are approximately three feet square or one meter square and are marked with floor tape. It is important to mark the boundaries of each gate with tape, as competitors are penalized for touching the lines during each pass through the course. The final section of the slalom is a series of turns (one to the left and two to the right) before finishing with a straight sprint. This final segment is also marked by directional arrows made of the floor tape. Competitors are only penalized for touching lines that mark the gate obstacles, not for touching directional arrows.

Starting the Game

The competitor must position their wheelchair so that the front tire is on the starting line. The start of the slalom is from a stationary position. The starter uses a starter's pistol and says, "Take your mark, set," and then fires the pistol. The competitor's time is recorded when the front tire of their wheelchair crosses the finish line.

Game Objective

The objective of the slalom event is to complete the course as fast as possible without accumulating penalty points or being disqualified. The competitor must follow the arrows and pass through the obstacles (gates) in the correct order. Penalty seconds will be assessed if the competitor completes the course out of sequence or skips an obstacle.

In an official event, three officials and two recorders are on the course to judge infractions. The competitor is assessed additional seconds for marker and line infractions. Any competitor who cannot finish the course due to mechanical failure will be disqualified.

Competitors must pay attention to the direction of travel. As they enter a reverse gate, they must be able to turn their wheelchairs 180 degrees in order to exit the opposite side of the gate. In other words, they exit the gate traveling backwards. As they exit traveling backwards, they again must turn their wheelchairs 180 degrees in order to travel forward into the next gate. Reverse gates are marked by white markers at the entrance and red markers at the exit. The circle marker is a single marker that the competitor must encircle completely before moving on to the next gate. The figure-eight gate has three markers set one meter apart in a straight line. To successfully complete the figure-eight gate, the competitor must weave between all three markers before moving to the next gate. The 360-degree gate is marked by four red markers, indicating that a complete turn must be executed inside the gate before exiting. The competitor enters and exits the 360-degree gate traveling forward.

Game Length

In an official competition, the only time constraint is enacted prior to the start of competition. The slalom is officially closed 15 minutes before the first race.

General Rules/Penalties

The slalom is a race against time. The competitor is penalized additional time for the following infractions or faults: (1) missing an obstacle, (2) knocking over a marker, (3) touching a line with a tire, and (4) touching a marker with the wheelchair or a body part.

If a competitor fails to follow the correct sequence of the course design, they must correct their mistake prior to entering the next obstacle. The competitor must correct this fault without assistance from coaches or teammates. Failure to correct this fault will result in a disqualification. For example, if a competitor skips an obstacle and realizes their mistake, they must return to the skipped obstacle prior to finishing the course.

Knocking over a marker results in a five-second penalty. The marker may not be replaced from where it was knocked down until the next competitor is ready to run through the course. If a marker gets caught underneath a wheelchair, it is up to the competitor to free the marker from the wheelchair. The competitor must remove the trapped marker by using wheelchair movements. No event official, coach, or teammate may assist in the removal of a trapped marker.

If the tire of the wheelchair touches a line of either the reverse or 360-degree gate, a three-second penalty is assessed. All maneuvers must be completed within the boundaries of each gate without touching the lines.

Touching a marker results in a three-second penalty to the competitor's total time. As the competitor moves into and out of each gate, they must concentrate on keeping their body position as stable as possible. If a competitor strikes a fallen marker, no additional penalty time is added.

Summary of the Sport

Table 8.1 will help you set up a slalom event for your students considered severely disabled. Although this event is designed for students with disabilities who use power or electric wheelchairs, students using manual wheelchairs can also participate.

Table 8.1	Overview of the Slalom
Field of play	Any hard, level surface, for example, tennis court, playground, track high jump takeoff area
Players	Students using power or electric wheelchairs, for example, those with severe CP, muscular dystrophy, spinal cord injury (quadriplegia), spina bifida, or other like conditions
Equipment	Floor tape; PVC pipe cut 16 in. tall by 4 in. diameter (26 pieces) or plastic bowling pins; strips of red cloth
Legal start	Stationary position at the starting line; front tires behind starting line; starter pistol is fired
Completing the course	Competitors must pass through the course as fast as possible, paying attention to the direction of travel and the type of obstacle (reverse gate, circle gate, 360-degree gate, figure-eight gate). Competitors must avoid body and wheelchair contact with taped lines and markers as they pass through the course. All reverse and 360 gates are 1 m square, and the figure-eight gate has three markers set 1 m apart.
Penalties and disqualifications	Skipping an obstacle (or not reentering in the correct order): Student is disqualified. Knocking over a marker: 5 sec Touching a line with a tire: 3 sec Touching a marker with the wheelchair or a body part: 3 sec

Skills to Be Taught

The slalom has four gate types that require specific maneuvers to negotiate: the reverse gate, the 360-degree gate, the figure-eight gate, and the circle gate. Only three maneuvers are used, however, because the circle gate (see p. 184) requires the same wheelchair movement as the 360-degree gate, only with a tighter turning radius. The three maneuvers require the student to control body position and the speed of the wheelchair, and accelerate and decelerate appropriately while negotiating an obstacle. Competition is traditionally conducted on a hard, flat, level outdoor surface, but students can practice these skills inside the gymnasium during your general physical education class.

Reverse Turn

Students should learn to identify a reverse gate before executing a reverse turn. The entrance to a reverse gate is marked with white markers indicating that the student must enter in a forward direction. The exit is marked by red markers, which requires the student to exit in a reverse direction. To negotiate this obstacle successfully, the student must have complete control of the wheelchair both entering and exiting.

To complete the reverse gate successfully, the student should enter in a forward direction and initiate a 180-degree turn as soon as possible once inside the gate, being careful to avoid line or marker infractions. The student should position the wheelchair directly in the center of the obstacle before turning. The student must know the length and width of their wheelchair and must maintain control. Once the 180-degree turn is complete, the student must exit the obstacle from the opposite side of entry. The students should look for landmarks or focal points to help with positioning and align the wheelchair before attempting the reverse exit. Once the reverse exit has taken place, they must again turn their wheelchair to a forward direction to continue through the course; another 180-degree turn is required as they head for the next obstacle.

Entering the reverse gate with white markers.

Inside the reverse gate.

Execute a 180-degree turn within the reverse gate, then exit backwards.

360-Degree Turn

The 360-degree turn is marked by four red markers at each corner. The student enters the gate with the same control as described for the reverse gate and positions the wheelchair in the center. To conduct the 360-degree maneuver, the student must have proper sitting posture and control of the toggle switch or joystick on the wheelchair. The student must turn the wheelchair one complete turn and exit from the opposite side of the point of entry facing in a forward direction. Remember, as the student turns the wheelchair within the obstacle, they must avoid touching the lines and markers. Touching lines or markers results in additional penalty seconds to their total elapsed time.

Enter a 360-degree gate facing forward.

Maintain body position; execute a complete turn within the gate.

Exit facing forward.

The circle gate.

Figure-Eight Turn

The student approaches the figure-eight gate in a forward direction and must weave through each of the three markers before moving to the next gate. The student should approach each marker ready to turn in the direction of most wheelchair control. For example, if the student has more control turning to the right, then they should approach the left side of the marker. Students who turn their wheelchair with more control to the left should approach the marker from the right side.

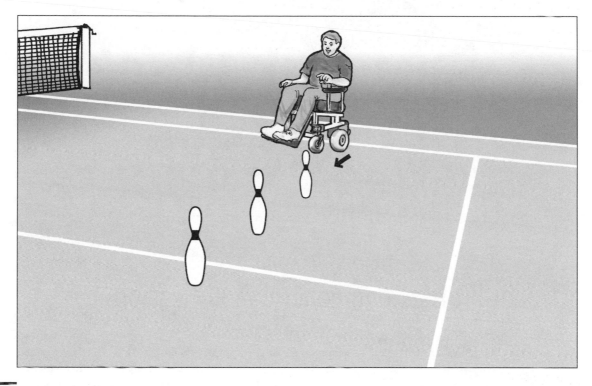

Approach the figure-eight gate with control.

Pass through, maintaining good sitting position.

Avoid touching markers.

Functional Profiles and General Modifications

The purpose of including the slalom in this book is to provide you with specific suggestions for your students with severe or multiple physical disabilities, in other words, those students with severe disabilities in at least three or all four extremities. Therefore, there is no section included for moderate- to high-functioning students *All suggested activities within this chapter are written for the student who uses a power or electric wheelchair independently.*

General Modifications

Table 8.2 offers suggestions for how you might apply general modifications to the three skills necessary to complete the slalom. As always, the students in your class and your teaching situation will determine your choice of modifications.

Table 8.2	General Modifications for the Slalom	
Skill level	**Skill**	**Activity modifications**
Low	Reverse turn	Enter the obstacle and back straight out without a reverse turn.
	360-degree turn	Enter the obstacle and change the direction of travel to exit (not necessarily a full 360-degree turn, e.g., quarter turn).
	Figure-eight turn	Weave around one marker rather than all three.

Game Progressions

Due to the independent nature of this event, it is difficult to apply small group and teamwork concepts to the suggested games. Nevertheless, some small group and teamwork activities are suggested to address motivation and practice for students with severe disabilities. These game progressions can also be used to address the three domains of learning in physical education: psychomotor, cognitive, and affective.

Games-by-Skill-Level Index

There will be only one games-by-skill-level index (table 8.3) for this chapter because the functional profile for this sport is low/severe. You will still cross-reference the skill by the level of activity you desire (individual, small group, or teamwork).

Table 8.3	Games-by-Skill-Level Index for Low-Functioning Students—The Slalom		
Skills	**Individual activity**	**Small group activity**	**Teamwork**
Reverse turn	Tap and Go	Grand Reverse	Reverse and Go
360-degree turn	Circle Up	Ring Masters	Reverse, Turn, and Go
Figure-eight turn	The Weave	Giant Slalom I	Giant Slalom II

Game Descriptions

The games are arranged according to skills and game level. Each game description includes game level, formation, equipment, description, extensions, and inclusion suggestions. You are free to decide the application of these games to your teaching situation.

Skill Reverse Turn

◆ Tap and Go

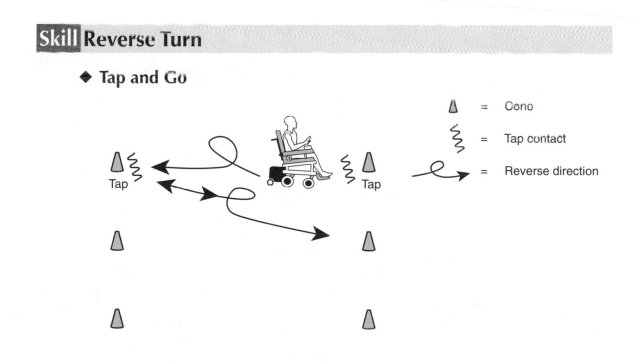

Game Level: Individual

Formation: Individual with peer assistant as needed

Equipment: Plastic bowling pins

Description: Place two sets of three plastic bowling pins on a line facing one another approximately 15 feet apart. Within sets, allow 10 feet between each bowling pin. The student starts in the middle of two sets facing the first pin of set 1. On command, the student moves their wheelchair forward, under control, and taps the first bowling pin (if it falls, that's OK). As the tap is made, the student reverses direction and spins 180 degrees to face the first pin of the second set. Again under control, the student moves forward and taps the pin, does a reverse spin, and moves on to the second pin of the first set. Tap and Go is continued until all pins have been tapped. You should emphasize wheelchair control and reversing directions.

Extension: Shorten the distance between the two sets of bowling pins, which will require additional control of the wheelchair.

Inclusion Suggestion: The student can demonstrate to the class their ability to accomplish the activity.

◆ Grand Reverse

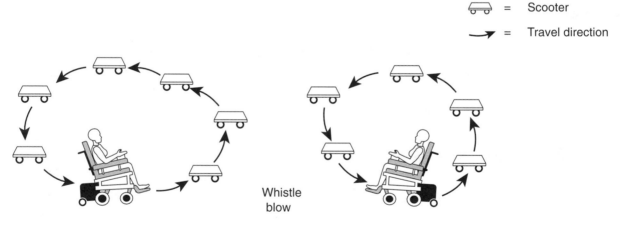

Game Level: Small group

Formation: Small groups of three or four students with and without disabilities in a circle formation

Equipment: Scooters, whistle

Description: Students are in three or four small groups in circle formations around the gym. Students without disabilities use scooters. The objective of the game is to have all the groups moving in a circular direction while facing the same direction (for example, forward). On the first whistle, everyone changes the direction they are facing but not the direction of travel. Make sure to allow enough space between students using scooters and students using power wheelchairs.

Extensions: Vary the activity by changing the frequency of the signals to change directions. Change the size of the circle. Include a ball in the activity and have students pass the ball with directional change.

Inclusion Suggestion: The student with a disability can initiate the change of direction.

◆ Reverse and Go

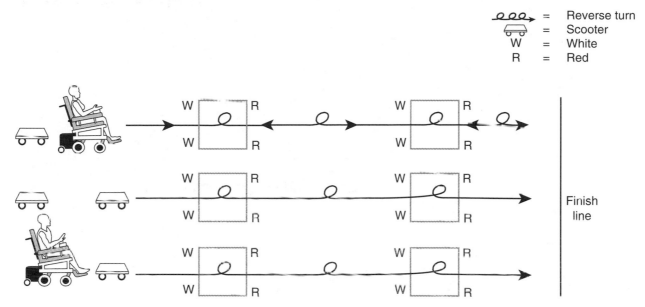

ꝏꝏꝏ→	=	Reverse turn
⛾	=	Scooter
W	=	White
R	=	Red

Game Level: Teamwork

Formation: The class is divided into three teams in preparation for a relay race.

Equipment: Plastic bowling pins (or equipment to make markers), floor tape, stopwatch

Description: Using the diagram from the official competition, set up six reverse gates (two per team) using red and white markers. Each reverse gate should measure one meter square and be marked with floor tape. Position each reverse gate four meters apart and allow 10 meters for a finishing distance. Line up each team behind their set of reverse gates and place students without disabilities on scooters. On the command to "go," each student travels to the first gate and performs a reverse movement inside the gate without touching any of the boundary lines. Once they have completed a reverse movement, they exit and continue to the next gate to repeat the movement. After they have completed the second reverse gate, students exit and sprint to the finish line. If a student touches a gate line, penalty seconds are added to their total time.

Extensions: Change the position of the students without disabilities on the scooters; for instance, they can complete the first trip seated, then change to a prone and then a kneeling position. Increase the number of reverse movements to be performed by those without disabilities (for instance, two reverses within each gate).

Inclusion Suggestion: The student with a disability can decide the position of travel for those students using scooters.

Skill 360-Degree Turn

◆ Circle Up

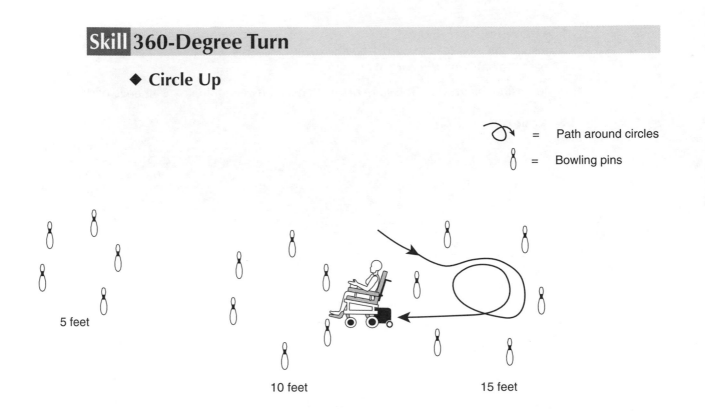

Game Level: Individual

Formation: Individual with peer assistant as needed

Equipment: Plastic bowling pins, traffic cones, floor tape

Description: Create three circles using plastic bowling pins or cones as boundaries. Each circle has a different diameter (for example, 15 feet, 10 feet, and 5 feet). Use the floor tape to mark the entrance and exit to and from the circle. The student moves their wheelchair forward into the circle and executes a complete 360-degree turn inside. Once they have completed the turn, they must find the exit arrow (floor tape) and exit the circle. The student must master one circle size before moving to the smaller size.

Extension: Challenge the student to move in succession from the 15-foot circle to the 10-foot to the 5-foot circle without stopping.

Inclusion Suggestions: The student can decide which circle to start with. Also, a student without disabilities can join using a scooter.

◆ Ring Masters

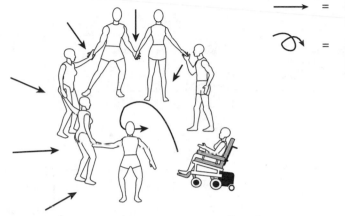

→ = Students making circle smaller

↻ = Path of student inside circle

Game Level: Small group

Formation: Small groups of three or four students with and without disabilities in a circle formation

Equipment: None required.

Description: Small groups of students create several circle formations around the gym. Students forming the circle should hold hands. The student with a disability is in the center of one circle (or more depending on the number in your class). On the signal to move, the student in the center of the circle moves their wheelchair around the inside circumference of the circle. On each pass around the circle the students move inward to create a smaller circle. The objective is to get the student in the center of the circle to turn 360 degrees in the smallest circle possible for their skill level.

Extension: At a signal to change direction, the student turns 360 degrees in the opposite direction as the circle continues to get smaller.

Inclusion Suggestions: The student with a disability can decide the starting circumference for each of the circles. Students without disabilities can participate by performing some form of locomotor movement around the circle (for example, hopping on one foot, sliding sideways, or bear or crab walking).

◆ Reverse, Turn, and Go

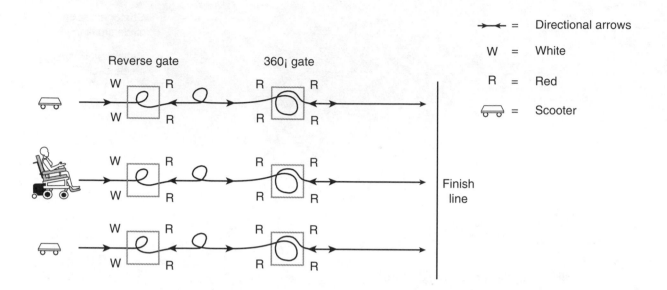

Game Level: Teamwork

Formation: The class is divided into three teams in preparation for a relay race.

Equipment: Plastic bowling pins (or equipment to make markers), floor tape, stopwatch

Description: Using the diagram from the official competition, set up three reverse gates and three 360-degree gates (one each per team) using red and white markers. Each gate should measure one meter square and be marked with floor tape. Position each gate four meters apart and allow 10 meters for a finishing distance. Line up each team behind their set of gates and place students without disabilities on scooters. On the command to "go," each student travels to the first gate and performs a reverse movement inside the gate without touching any of the boundary lines. Once they have completed a reverse movement, they exit and continue to the next gate to complete a full 360-degree turn inside the gate. They then exit and sprint to the finish line. If a student touches a gate line, penalty seconds are added to their total time.

Extensions: Change the position of the students without disabilities on the scooters; for example, on their first trip they may sit, then change to a front-lying or kneeling position. If scooters are not available for students without disabilities, have these students perform various locomotor movements as they participate in the relay race, such as hopping on one foot or jumping with two feet.

Inclusion Suggestion: The student with a disability can decide the order of the course (for example, the 360-degree gate first, then the reverse gate).

Skill Figure-Eight Turn

◆ The Weave

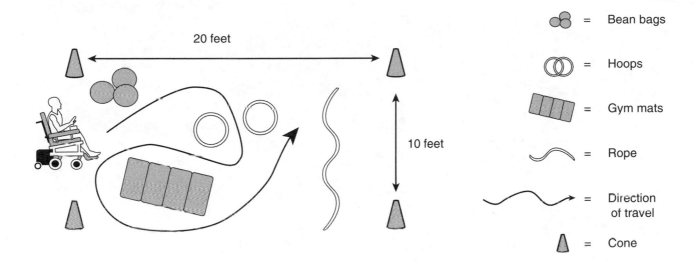

Game Level: Individual

Formation: Individual with peer assistant as needed.

Equipment: Various pieces of equipment scattered about the game area, such as beanbags, hoops, gym mats, rope

Description: Scatter several pieces of equipment randomly on the floor within a small game area (e.g., 10 feet by 20 feet). On the signal, the student begins moving within the game area, avoiding contact with the equipment. The student should move left and right as they weave through the game area in figure-eight patterns.

Extensions: Increase the number of pieces of equipment within the area. Challenge the student to move from one end of the game area to the opposite end as fast as possible.

Inclusion Suggestions: A classmate without a disability can move on a scooter through the course at the same time as the student with a disability. The student with a disability can scatter the pieces of equipment and adjust the distances between each piece. The student with a disability can also decide the scooter position for the student without a disability (for instance, kneeling, sitting, prone).

◆ Giant Slalom I

= Weave

= Run direction

= Pins

Game Level: Small group

Formation: Students stand in small groups around a circle of bowling pins. A student with a disability is in the center of the circle.

Equipment: Plastic bowling pins or small traffic cones

Description: Students are in small groups of three or four. The student with a disability is in the center of a circle of bowling pins (at least 12 pins about six feet apart). Students without disabilities stand outside the circle of bowling pins. On a signal the student with a disability moves from the center and begins weaving in and out of the bowling pins as the students without disabilities move around the circle. After one trip around the circle, the student returns to the center and calls out a classmate's name. The student who is called moves to the center of the circle, tags the first student, and then moves around the circle, weaving in and out of the bowling pins. The game continues until all students have completed a turn around the circle. Once each group has had an opportunity to practice, repeat the game for time, remembering to enforce any penalty times for touching or knocking over the bowling pins.

Extensions: Increase the number of bowling pins or traffic cones to pass, or decrease the distance between each cone for the weave. Set up the same game using a straight-line formation.

Inclusion Suggestion: Students without disabilities can use scooters or some form of alternative locomotor movement, such as skipping or hopping on one foot.

◆ **Giant Slalom II**

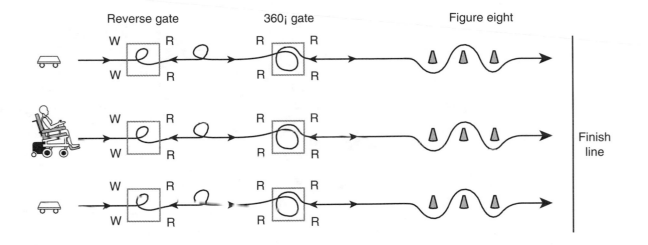

Game Level: Teamwork

Formation: The class is divided into three teams in preparation for a relay race.

Equipment: Plastic bowling pins (or equipment to make markers), floor tape, stopwatch

Description: Using the diagram from the official competition, set up three reverse gates, three 360-degree gates, and three figure-eight gates (one each per team) using red and white markers. Each gate should measure one meter square and be marked with floor tape. Each of the three markers for the figure-eight gate should be one meter apart. Position each gate four meters apart and allow 10 meters for a finishing distance. Line up each team behind their set of gates and place students without disabilities on scooters. On the command to "go," each student travels through the course, completing passes through the reverse, 360-degree, and figure-eight gates as fast as possible. You may want to enforce penalty seconds to their total time if a student touches a gate line.

Extensions: Change the position of the students without disabilities on the scooters; for instance, on their first trip they may sit, then change to a front-lying or kneeling position on subsequent trips. If scooters are not available for students without disabilities, these students can perform various locomotor movements as they participate in the relay race (for example, hopping on one foot or jumping with two feet).

Inclusion Suggestion: The student with a disability can decide the order for completing the course (for example, reverse gate first, then the figure-eight gate, and finish with the 360-degree gate).

appendix

A

Legal Applications

Improving Services

To improve educational services for your students with disabilities, you, as the general physical educator, need to become directly involved with the IEP (individualized education plan) process. You can best accomplish this by (1) communicating with special educators and other teachers; (2) assessing students with disabilities; and (3) contributing present-level statements, annual goals, and short-term objectives to the IEP.

Improving Communication— With Whom?

You need to establish communication lines with several professionals within your school building. The special education classroom teacher, physical and/or occupational therapist(s), adapted physical educator, and school nurse can offer specific information that can be applied to sound physical education programming for your student with a disability. Keep in mind that communication is bidirectional: you must talk to them, and they must talk to you.

The special education classroom teacher will be able to share information about academic strengths and weaknesses such as reading levels. This information can help you plan units that require keeping score or keeping track of team win/loss records.

The physical/occupational therapists will be able to share motor information related to functional performance, reflex development or interference, and daily living or lifetime skills. These professionals should be able to help you determine appropriate activities that your students with disabilities might need later in life, such as trunk stability or arm/shoulder strength.

The adapted physical educator will be able to address activity modifications and motor assessment issues related to physical education activities. The adapted physical educator generally fills the role of direct service provider or school district consultant. In either role increases the opportunity for this professional will cross your path. Often you will both attend departmental meetings on issues surrounding physical education in general, such as curriculum development or parent meetings. As these opportunities arise, take the time to initiate conversations regarding programming for students with disabilities that might include information concerning the IEP process. The adapted physical educator will also be versed in the type and severity of the student's disability, which will help you select appropriate physical education activities.

The school nurse can be helpful on a daily basis with activities such as the administration of medication, catheterization, and the daily well-being of the student with a disability. The school nurse is often the individual who has all the medical records for the student in question and is generally in frequent communication with the student's parents.

Improving Communication—How?

The lack of communication between the special education classroom teacher and the physical educator often has to do with school building logistics. Ask yourself, where is the special education classroom(s) in my building related to the gymnasium? The two are often on opposite ends of the building, separated by administrative offices, the library, and/or the cafeteria. Transition from classroom to classroom is another limitation for communication. Rarely do students with disabilities change classroom settings once the school day has begun, and neither do their teachers. Teachers are often isolated throughout the day, having minimal interaction time with their colleagues. Teachers need to seek ways to enhance communication.

One method to facilitate communication probably already exists in your building. You and your special education colleagues probably share several activities that could foster informal meetings throughout your school day. These meetings usually take place in the teacher's lounge, hallways, or during preparation times. If these opportunities do not exist within your regular daily schedule, you might want to consider scheduling a breakfast meeting before school with your special education colleague. Another method to help facilitate communication is to schedule your lunch or preparation times with your special education classroom teacher. Face-to-face discussions are most helpful, but if they are not possible, technology might be the best method for you and your colleagues.

With the prominence of electronic mail, or e-mail, information exchange has been greatly enhanced. By using e-mail, you and your special education colleague might be able to exchange information outside of the school schedule. Information such as assessment results, scheduled parent–teacher meetings, or IEP meetings might be included in these e-mail exchanges. E-mailed information could be sent from within your school building or between two different buildings. If your special education colleague is aware of any students who might be transferring to your building, an e-mail announcing such an event might be very helpful to you. Prior notice would allow you to secure important background information on the student before their arrival.

If your school does not offer e-mail, then interoffice memos and/or facsimile (faxing) might be the best method for you. In order for interoffice memos or faxes to be effective, you will need to develop a simple form to be exchanged between you and the special educator. The form could include pertinent information about the student, such as name, grade, goals/objectives, strengths, weaknesses, likes and dislikes, and behavior reinforcers. You can exchange interoffice memos through faculty mailboxes.

Improving Communication—When?

Most special education administrative activities (case conferences, IEP meetings, etc.) are scheduled around the beginning and end of the school calendar. Many school districts plan their special education progress meetings for the end of the school year and their evaluation or assessment activities for the beginning of the school year. However, teachers need to exchange student progress information more frequently.

Daily communication between you and your special education colleague concerning the programming issues of a student with a disability would be ideal. Being able to learn new developments from each other would help with the overall development of the student. However, since daily e-mails, faxes, and interoffice communications are difficult to manage, you might consider weekly exchanges. Whether you have established an electronic mode of communication or more traditional modes, even weekly updates would enhance programming considerations for the student in question.

Contributing to the Assessment Process

Educational placement decisions regarding students with disabilities in physical education need to be based on a comprehensive assessment in physical education. An assessment practice that addresses the student's individual needs in physical and motor fitness; fundamental motor skills; and skills needed to participate in individual and group games, sports, aquatics, and dance must be conducted. Both PL 94-142 and PL 105-17 mandate that such assessments be conducted by a trained professional. With decisions such as educational placement to be considered, historically that trained professional was an adapted physical educator. If a trained adapted physical educator is not available in your school or school district, you, the general physical educator, will need to complete this assessment. To facilitate future sport/recreational opportunities, you will need to start by asking a series of questions that might help determine such opportunities and contribute to the overall assessment process. For example, questions in the following categories might be asked:

- *Background*. What is the type and severity of the disability?
- *Opportunities*. What sports or recreational opportunities presently exist in the community or will exist once this student completes high school?
- *Logistics*. What are the logistical and transportation concerns related to participating in a sport or recreational activity outside of school?
- *Skills needed*. What opportunities exist in the current physical education curriculum to develop appropriate sport/recreational/leisure skills for the future? Which of these skills are needed to successfully participate in the future?

Using Criterion-Referenced Assessment

Once these questions have been addressed, the information from this text could help you conduct a skill analysis using a criterion-referenced approach. Here the student's performance is compared to a set of descriptors or criteria as they perform a given movement. For example, the following criteria might be used to assess throwing a ball using an overhand motion for a student without a disability:

- Stands with side orientation to the target.
- Holds ball in throwing hand.
- Brings ball back with throwing arm, elbow bent.
- Rotates trunk at waist in preparation to throw.
- Brings ball backward, forward, and overhead, and rotates trunk toward direction of target upon ball release.
- Releases ball, follows through, and shifts weight to maintain balance.

With each phase of the movement, the student is compared to the criteria to see how well they perform the skill. Since you are trained to recognize movement and have the ability to analyze movement skills, conducting a criteria assessment for a student with a disability is the same process. For example, after reading the skill breakdowns presented in this book, you have the ability to create your own criteria assessment for a student with a disability.

Using This Text for Assessment

Let's say you have set a goal for a student to play wheelchair basketball in a recreational league by high school graduation. After responding to the previous set of questions, you would have to determine the essential basketball skills this student would need by graduation. In chapter 3 on wheelchair basketball, you read that there are several skills specific to wheelchair basketball (that is, the pass, dribble, shoot, bounce stop, bounce spin, and ball retrieval).

Each skill is broken down into teaching points, or criteria of movement (skill analysis). For example, the bounce stop has four key teaching points:

- Bounce the ball to the side of the wheelchair.
- Grab both handrims as the ball hits the floor.
- Pull back with hands to stop wheelchair.
- Catch ball after stopping as ball rebounds from floor.

By transferring these criteria to an assessment checklist (a form of criterion assessment) and adding a quantitative measure, you can create an assessment tool that will help you teach and help you and your student with a disability achieve the goal of playing in a recreational league after graduation.

Creating Your Own Assessment

Table A.1 illustrates how the information presented for the bounce stop can be used to create an assessment using criteria from the teaching points.

To use this table, place a check mark in the box that represents the appropriate level of performance each time the student is tested. Repeat the same assessment approach

Table A.1	Criterion Assessment for Bounce Stop in Wheelchair Basketball			
	Student's name: _____			
Skill	Teaching points (skill analysis)	1 of 3 times	2 of 3 times	3 of 3 times
Bounce stop	1. Bounce the ball to the side of the wheelchair.			
	2. Grab both handrims as the ball hits the floor.			
	3. Pull back with hands to stop the wheelchair.			
	4. Catch the ball after stopping as the ball rebounds from the floor.			

for the other skills that would be appropriate for the student(s) with disabilities to accomplish within wheelchair basketball or any other sport skill. Please note that all the skills in wheelchair basketball may not be possible for all students with disabilities to accomplish, which is acceptable. Remember, you are trying to choose the skills that will allow this student to participate in wheelchair basketball safely and successfully now and in the future. Some students with disabilities might only be able to accomplish the pass and shoot, whereas others might be able to accomplish the pass, dribble, shoot, and bounce stop. Each student is different, and each brings their own unique set of abilities. Once you have assessed, you are ready to contribute to the IEP by writing present-level statements, annual goals, and short-term objectives.

Contributing to the IEP

In order to become more involved with the IEP process, you should improve your knowledge of at least three basic components of an IEP: the present-level statement, the annual goal, and short-term objectives. These components are central to the IEP document and the educational placement for least restrictive environment. Using examples from chapter 3, "Wheelchair Basketball," and chapter 7, "Goalball," let's look at how each of these IEP components could be applied.

Present Level of Performance

The present-level performance statement is written based on an assessment of what the child can do. Notice the emphasis is on "can." The present-level performance statement should not tell someone what the child *can't* do but what they are accomplishing at the present time. Here are two examples of how to write a present-level statement using the information from this book.

Let's say Tony is an eighth-grader who uses a wheelchair and you have him in a basketball unit. Tony is moderate to high functioning and has the potential to play competitive wheelchair basketball in the future. One of the skills you should assess is the bounce stop, which is a skill that Tony has some difficulty with. Using an assessment chart you created from the teaching points of the bounce stop, you write the following present-level statement for Tony:

Present-Level Statement: Tony can complete two bounce stops in wheelchair basketball.

The second example concerns a student with a visual impairment. Andrea is in the sixth grade and is considered legally blind. You would like Andrea to learn the game of goalball, so you conduct an assessment of her skills. One of the skills needed for goalball is blocking from a standing position. However, Andrea is only able to block from her knees. Your present-level statement for her might read as follows:

Present-Level Statement: Andrea can block a rolled goalball from a kneeling position.

Annual Goals

Annual goals have been explained as looking at the big picture. They are generally written from a broader perspective and are not meant to be quantified. Continuing with our two students, their annual goal statements might read as follows:

Annual Goal: Tony will improve his wheelchair basketball skills.

Annual Goal: Andrea will improve her skills in goalball.

Short-Term Objectives

Short-term objectives are the "stair steps" leading to the annual goal and should be written in measurable context (that is, quantifiably). Although the concept of "measurable" is often left to interpretation by each school district, it is generally considered that unit measurement of distance, weight, or time is acceptable for physical education. Some measurement statements are written as a percentage of accomplishments (for example, three of five trials, or 60 percent). Short-term objectives for Tony and Andrea might be written in the following manner:

1. ***Tony will be able to complete three of five attempts of the bounce stop in 30 seconds.***
2. ***Tony will be able to complete five of five attempts of the bounce stop in 30 seconds.***
1. ***Andrea will be able to block a rolled goalball from a standing position in three of six attempts.***
2. ***Andrea will be able to block a rolled goalball from a standing position in six of six attempts.***

Notice that each short-term objective should move you in the direction of accomplishing the annual goal and improving the present level of performance statement. Thus, the interpretation for Tony would be that if Tony completed three out of five bounce stops and then five out of five bounce stops within 30 seconds, he would be moving toward meeting his annual goal of improving his wheelchair basketball skills (see Table A.2).

Table A.2	Sample IEP Using Only Three Components
Student information	Name: Tony Grade: 8th School: East Wing MS
Present level of performance	Tony can complete two bounce stops in wheelchair basketball.
Annual goal	Tony will improve his wheelchair basketball skills.
Short-term objectives	1. Tony will be able to complete 3 of 5 attempts of the bounce stop in 30 seconds. 2. Tony will be able to complete 5 of 5 attempts of the bounce stop in 30 seconds.

Summary

The purpose of this section is to help you become involved with the legal mandates for the child with a disability in physical education. You can do so by improving your communication with your special education colleagues, contributing to the assessment process of students with disabilities, and actively engaging in the IEP development. The information presented in this text should help you accomplish all three.

appendix

B

Wheelchair Basics

Four sports presented in this book require the use of a wheelchair: wheelchair basketball, indoor wheelchair soccer, wheelchair tennis, and the slalom. Students who use wheelchairs often know more than their teachers about the operation and maintenance of the wheelchair. The purpose of this section is to provide a brief overview of how to purchase and care for this important piece of equipment. By knowing more about your students' wheelchairs, you will be in a better position to discuss this topic with your school district's physical or occupational therapists or answer questions from parents. Remember the wheelchair is an important piece of equipment for your students with disabilities. The more knowledge you have about this equipment, the more informative you can be in your job. Increasing your knowledge of the wheelchair will help normalize the piece of equipment to your students without disabilities. By demonstrating how much you know about the wheelchair, you help set the atmosphere and attitude for your classes. Learning more about the wheelchair also provides you an opportunity to teach others and reduce stereotyping of students with disabilities who use this equipment to move.

The first step in selecting a wheelchair is to consult with the local physical or occupational therapist in your school district. These professionals are trained to conduct measurements for proper fit and selection. You may also follow the measuring tips suggested later in this section. Beyond proper fit, you should be able to determine the correct wheelchair type, frame design, and general size for your student.

Wheelchair Types

Wheelchairs fall into two basic categories: manual and power. Manual wheelchairs are those that are propelled by the individual, whereas power wheelchairs are powered by a battery and motor. Only manual wheelchairs will be discussed here in detail because you are more likely to encounter a student using one. However, should one of your students use a power wheelchair, make sure you have the student show you two key features: how to operate the on/off switch and how to disengage the clutch. Not all manufacturers put the on/off switch in the same location. Make sure your student shows you where this switch is and how it functions. Do likewise for the clutch mechanism. Releasing the clutch allows you to move the power wheelchair when the power is off. This comes in handy when maneuvering in tight spaces or on pool decks. Always turn the power off and disengage the clutch when operating a power wheelchair on a pool deck.

Manual wheelchairs are offered in several designs: standard, ultralight (also known as sports competition), and racing.

Standard wheelchairs are best described as those found in hospitals. They are usually made of stainless steel and constructed for durability. The average weight of a standard wheelchair is approximately 50 pounds or more. These wheelchairs are usually equipped with removable armrests and footplates and have limited adjustments to seating. The tires are usually tubeless and made of hard rubber mounted on spoked wheels about 27 inches or more in diameter. The front tires, or casters, are generally 3.5 to 5 inches in diameter and are also made of tubeless, hard rubber. These wheelchairs can be used indoors or outdoors and can be maneuvered over many different surfaces such as asphalt, cement, and wood floors.

Ultralights, or sports competition wheelchairs, are designed for activities that require quick response and fast-paced action. These wheelchairs are made of lightweight metal alloys and usually weigh between 15 and 20 pounds. Many dimensions on these wheelchairs are adjustable, including the seat position, back height, foot carriage, seat angle, and camber of the mainwheels. They generally do not have armrests or footplates unless specially ordered. The camber is the "flaring out" of the mainwheels as you view the wheelchair from the rear. Camber is important for ultralight wheelchairs, as it contributes to maneuverability.

The front casters on ultralights are generally very small, approximately three inches in diameter, and often are the same wheels as those used on in-line skates. Since these wheelchairs are designed to be used indoors on a basketball court or outdoors on a tennis court, there is an increased likelihood of dirt and grime building up in the bearings of the front casters. The front casters should receive regular scheduled maintenance, which includes cleaning the axles and bearings.

Another feature of the ultralight wheelchair is the pop-off wheels, which aid in repair issues or ease of transportation. A button at the center of the mainwheel axle, which is a solid piece of metal at the center hub, releases the wheel and tire assembly from the frame with one movement. When the button is pushed, the entire tire assembly can be removed and a backup tire assembly can be mounted. Once the tire assembly is removed from the wheelchair frame, the button can be pressed again to remove the axle from the hub for replacement or repairs.

Push the button to release the wheel from the frame.

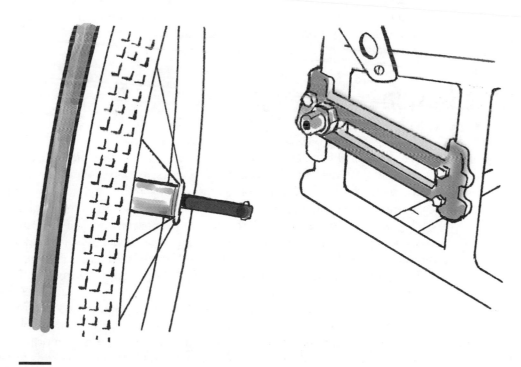

Remove the wheel from the frame.

Push the button again to remove the axle from the wheel.

Racing wheelchairs are manufactured specifically for road races or track events. These wheelchairs are generally longer in the wheelbase and much lighter in weight than the ultralight wheelchairs. Racing wheelchairs are custom fit for the individual with regard to seating position. The individual actually sits in a form-fitted cage or "bucket" area that has been precisely measured for hip width. Several models have a steering mechanism for the front casters to help negotiate the road or track courses. Racing wheelchairs are a much greater financial investment than either of the other two models. It is not uncommon for an individual to pay over $2,500 U.S. for this type of wheelchair.

Frame Design

Frame designs come in two basic models: folding and solid. Folding frames are found with standard wheelchairs, which are manufactured to fold in half by collapsing down the middle. This feature allows for ease of portability; that is, it can be folded to fit into the trunk of a car. In addition to the folding frame style, most standard wheelchairs feature removable footplates, which can help with storage or transportation issues.

Ultralight wheelchairs are of solid frame construction. These frames are not designed to collapse for transportation or storage. The advantage of solid frame construction has to do with reaction forces. The solid frame wheelchair is better designed to "push back" or react when a person applies a high degree of force, such as during manual propulsion. Since the frame is solid, it is less likely to absorb the force than a folding wheelchair. Think about sitting in a solid kitchen chair versus a soft couch. Which chair do you have an easier time rising from? The soft couch absorbs your forces as you push against it to stand, whereas the solid kitchen chair does not; in principle, it pushes back to help you rise more easily. You might simply ask your student, "Is that a solid frame or a folding frame?"

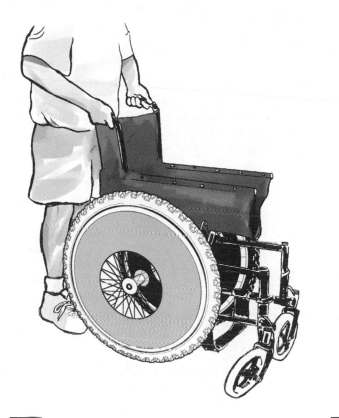

Positioning the folding wheelchair.

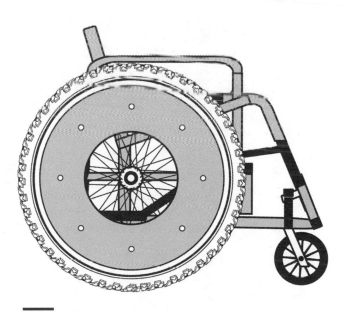

Opening the folding wheelchair.

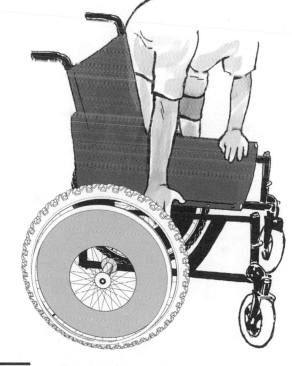

Stabilizing the folding wheelchair.

Solid frame sports competition wheelchair.

Wheelchair Fitting

Buying a wheelchair is as individualized as buying shoes. Each of us has unique foot characteristics that must be addressed when purchasing shoes: long and narrow, short and wide, short and narrow, and so on. The specific measurements of the individual's body must be taken into account when fitting them for a wheelchair. Basic anatomical measurements of the user must be taken regardless of whether you are purchasing a standard or an ultralight wheelchair.

The following are suggestions for measuring someone who is considering purchasing a wheelchair. Use these as guidelines, but seek the expertise of the school district therapist or a representative from a retail wheelchair distributor to help you with conducting the measurements. *Remember to take all measurements on an individual who is in a seated position.*

- **Shoulder.** Measure from the top of the shoulder to the palm of the hand with the arm extended in front of the body, and from the top of the shoulder to the seat.
- **Leg.** To measure leg length, measure the length of the upper leg from the hip center to the knee joint, and measure the lower leg length from the knee joint to the footrest.
- **Hips (seat).** For seat length, or seat depth, measure from behind the knee joint to the back of the seat, and for seat width, measure laterally from hip to hip.
- **Back.** For back height, measure from the seat base upward depending on the type of disability. Individuals with lower spinal cord injuries or injuries to the lumbar region will have lower seat-back heights, whereas individuals with injuries in the upper thoracic region will need higher seat-back support.

You may want to refer to table B.1 for an overview of how to fit a person to a wheelchair.

Table B.1	Measuring Guide for Fitting a Wheelchair
Body part	**Measurements (from a seated position)**
Shoulder	Top of shoulder to palm of hand with arm extended in front of body Top of shoulder to seat
Leg	Length of upper leg from center of hip to knee joint Length of lower leg from knee joint to footrest
Hips (seat)	Seat length or depth: Measure from behind the knee joint to the back of the seat Seat width: Measure from hip to hip
Back	Measure from seat base upward depending on type of disability. Individuals with lower spinal cord injuries (lower lumbar region) will have lower seat-back heights. Individuals with higher injuries (upper thoracic) will need higher seat-back support.

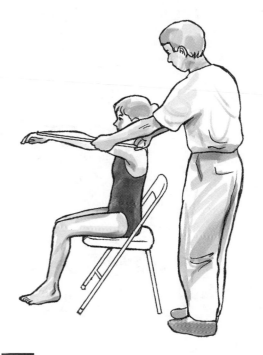

Shoulder measurement, arm forward.

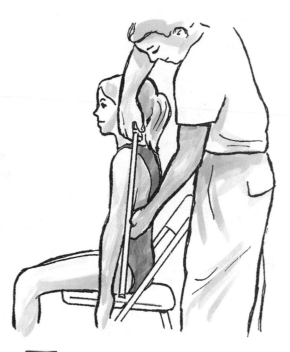

Shoulder measurement, arm down.

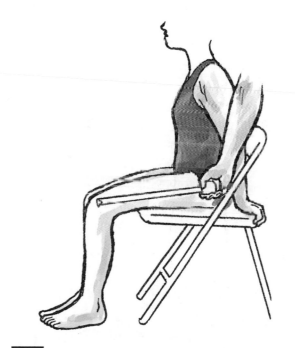

Leg measurement, upper leg.

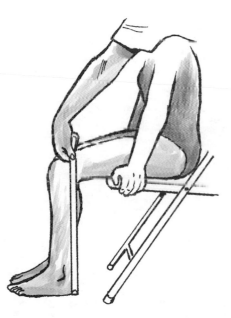

Leg measurement, lower leg.

Seat-depth measurement.

Seat-width measurement.

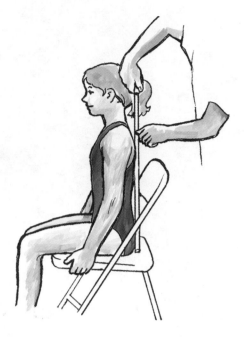

Seat-back height measurement.

appendix

C

Links to Other Sports and Adapted Activities

Web Sites for Disability Sports

Wheelchair Basketball
National Wheelchair Basketball Association: **http://www:nwba.org**
Indoor Wheelchair Soccer
National Disability Sports Alliance: **http://www.ndsaonline.org**
(Formerly known as the United States Cerebral Palsy Athletic Association)
Sitting Volleyball
World Organization of Volleyball for the Disabled: **http://www.wovd.com**
Wheelchair Tennis
International Federation of Tennis: **http://www.itftennis.com**
Goalball
United States Association of Blind Athletes: **http://www.usaba.org**
The Slalom
National Disability Sports Alliance: **http://www.ndsaonline.org**

Other Sport Contacts

Special Olympics
http://www.specialolympics.org
General Wheelchair Sports
http://www.wsusa.org
Deaf Sports
http://www.usadsf.org
Wheelchair Racquetball
http://www.usra.org

Adapted Physical Education Web Sites

PE Central
http://www.pe.central.vt.edu
Adapted Physical Education National Standards
http://www.twu.edu.apens
PALAESTRA: Forum for Sport, Physical Education, Recreation for those with Disabilities
http://www.palaestra.com

D

Equipment Concerns

Not everyone has a large budget to purchase some of the specialized pieces of equipment used in certain disability sports. Equipment purchases such as wheelchairs, goalballs, and special rackets can be costly. Here are a few suggestions to help you address this issue.

Wheelchairs

Having additional wheelchairs will help you implement some of the activities suggested in this book and help you create more inclusive settings. The following suggestions are offered to help you secure wheelchairs for your physical education classes:

- Contact your local medical supply store, hospital, or rehabilitation center to see if you might be able to borrow the wheelchairs for the duration of a particular unit—for instance, a two-week wheelchair basketball unit.
- Check the Internet for wheelchair manufacturers that might sell refurbished wheelchairs at a reduced cost.
- Check with the physical or occupation therapist at your school to see if they know how you might arrange the use of several wheelchairs.

Goalballs

To purchase a regulation goalball, contact the United States Association for Blind Athletes (USABA). If you do not have the funds to purchase a goalball, you can make your own using an old basketball. Here's how:

- Cut a small hole about three to five inches long in the basketball.
- Stuff the basketball with old newspapers or packing foam particles. Allow enough room to include three large jingle bells that can be purchased from a local craft store.
- Once stuffed, secure the opening with packing tape. You are now ready to play the game.

Wheelchair Tennis

For students who are unable to hold a regulation tennis racket or racquetball racket, you can make a modified racket from a wire coat hanger and an old pair of women's panty hose.

- Stretch the coat hanger from its original shape to one more like a diamond by pulling the lower bar down and away from the top or hook.
- Once the coat hanger is approximately 8 to 10 inches long, cut the foot portion of the panty hose about 10 inches above the base of the foot.
- Turn the coat hanger upside down and hold it by the hook. Slip the entire coat hanger into the panty hose and secure the end of the hose near the hook with a piece of masking tape or rubber bands. The nylon mesh serves as the webbing of the modified tennis racket. For safety, bend the curve of the hook up and in and secure it with masking tape to reduce sharp edges.

Suggested Readings

Many of the suggestions presented in this book have come from ideas generated by reading the following books. While much of the information found in *Inclusion Through Sports* is the result of professional experience, these suggested readings should offer you valuable support.

Auxter, D., J. Pyfer, and C. Huettig. 2001. *Principles and methods of adapted physical education and recreation.* 9th ed. Boston: WCB McGraw-Hill.

Davis, R., M. Ferrara, and D. Byrnes. 1988. The competitive wheelchair stroke. *National Strength and Conditioning Journal* 10(3): 4-10.

DePauw, K., and S. Gavron. 1995. *Disability and sport.* Champaign, IL: Human Kinetics.

Hedrick, B., D. Byrnes, and L. Shaver. 1994. *Wheelchair basketball.* 2nd ed. Washington, DC: Paralyzed Veterans of America.

Jones, J. 1988. *Training guide to cerebral palsy sports.* 3rd ed. Champaign, IL: Human Kinetics.

Kasser, L. S. 1995. *Inclusive games: Movement fun for everyone!* Champaign, IL: Human Kinetics.

Lieberman, L., and J. Cowart. 1996. *Games for people with sensory impairments. Strategies for including individuals of all ages.* Champaign, IL: Human Kinetics.

Moore, B., and R. Snow. 1994. *Wheelchair tennis. Myth to reality.* Dubuque, IA: Kendall/Hunt.

Paciorek, M., and J. Jones. 2001. *Disability sport and recreation resources.* 3rd ed. Traverse City, MI: Cooper Publishing Group.

Shephard, R. 1990. *Fitness in special populations.* Champaign, IL: Human Kinetics.

Sherrill, C. 1998. *Adapted physical activity, recreation and sport: Crossdisciplinary and lifespan.* 5th ed. Boston: WCB McGraw-Hill.

United States Association for Blind Athletes. 2000. *Sports rules: Goalball.* United States Association for Blind Athletes, 33 North Institute Street, Colorado Springs, CO.

United States Cerebral Palsy Athletic Association (USCPAA). 1997. *Sports rules manual.* 5th ed. Newport, RI: USCPAA.

World Organization Volleyball for Disabled (WOVD). 2000. *Sitting volleyball rules.* WOVD Headquarters, Klein Heiligland 90, NL-2011 EJ Haarlem, Lindelaan 3: The Netherlands.

Index

Page locators followed by an italicized *t* indicate information contained in tables.

A

adapted physical education Web sites 214
adapted physical educators 197, 198, 199
annual goals 202*t*
assessment 5, 199-201*t*
At the Hoop 48

B

Balloon Backhand 140
Beat the Clock 76
Block It 172
Bump and Go I 75
Bump and Go II 75-76

C

Call It Out 46, 82-83
Capture It 72
Charge! 73
Child Find 4-5
Circle Up 190
Clean the Kitchen 122-123
communication with teachers/professionals 197-199
Crossover 52-53

D

deaf sports Web site 214
Delivery Service 142
disability assessment 199-201*t*
disability categories 4
Don't Go There I 164
Don't Go There II 165
Don't Go There III 165-166
Down and Back 55

E

Education for All Handicapped Children Act (PL 94-142) 3-4, 199
e-mail 198-199
equipment 216

F

Feed and Go 84, 89
Feed and Go Plus 1 84, 89-90
Feed Me 83
Four Square 173

G

Gauntlet I 37-38
Gauntlet II 38
Gauntlet III 39
Giant Slalom I 194
Giant Slalom II 195
Giddy Up 55-56
Give and Go 33
goalball
    about 151-157
    blocking skills 158-159, 164-166, 171-173
    equipment 216
    game descriptions for low-functioning students 162*t*-167
    game descriptions for moderate-to high-functioning students 168*t*-175
    games by skill-level 162*t*, 168*t*
    modifications 161*t*
    passing skills 159-160, 166-167, 173-175
    student functional profiles 160-161*t*
    throwing skills 157-158, 162-164, 168-170
    Web sites 214
Grand Reverse 188-189
Guest Server 142-143

H

Hanging On 33
Here I Am 166, 173-174

I

inclusion 5-6
individualized education plans (IEPs) 5-6, 197, 201-202*t*
indoor wheelchair soccer
    about 57-62*t*, 60*t*
    blocking skills 67-68, 79-80, 89-90
    dribbling skills 65-66, 75-76, 85-86
    game descriptions for low-functioning students 70*t*-80
    game descriptions for moderate-to high-functioning students 81*t*-90
    games by skill-level 70*t*, 81*t*
    modifications for 69*t*-70
    passing skills 62-65, 71-72, 81-83

shooting skills 73-74, 83-84
    student functional profiles 69*t*-70
    throw-in 66-67, 77-78, 87-89
    Web sites 214
In the Bucket 47

J

Just the Three of Us 121

K

Keep It In 111-112
Keep It Out I 79
Keep It Out II 79-80
Keep It Out III 80
Knock It Off I 77
Knock It Off II 77-78
Knock It Off III 78

L

least restrictive environment (LRE) 5-6

M

memos 199
Mixed Doubles Plus 1 146-147

O

occupational therapists 197, 198
On the Move I 49-50, 85-86
On the Move II 50, 86
Over It Goes 114

P

Partner Pass 82
Pass and Shoot 35, 36-37
Pass It On I 71
Pass It On II 71
Pass It Up 115
physical therapists 197, 198, 205
Pick a Spot 87-88
Pick a Spot With "D" 88-89
Pin Block 89
present-level performance statement 201-202*t*
Put 'em Up 119-120

R

Reach Back 87
Reach for It 54

Reaching Out I 42
Reaching Out II 42-43
Reaching Out III 43
Rebound 73-74
Remember Me 45
Remember Me I 166-167
Remember Me II 174
Reverse, Turn, and Go 192
Reverse and Go 144-145, 189
Right Back at You 36, 110-111
Ring Masters 191
Rip It 118-119
Roll and Block I 111

S

school nurses 197, 198
Score It 74
The Serving Chair 147
Serving Cone 112-113
Serving Line 113
Serving Math 123
Serving the Reverse and Go 145-146
short-term objectives 202t
Shot's Away 34-35
sitting volleyball
    about 93-98, 97t
    attack-hit (kill) 100-101, 108-110,
        117-119
    blocking 102-103, 110-112, 119-
        121
    game descriptions for low-
        functioning students 105-114,
        106t
    game descriptions for moderate-
        to high-functioning students
        114-123, 115t
    games by skill-level 106t, 115t
    modifications 104-105t
    passing (setting) 98-100, 106-108,
        115-117
    serving 103-104, 112-114, 121-123
    student functional profiles 104t
    Web sites 214
skills assessments 200-201t
The Slalom
    about 177-180t
    figure-eight turns 184-186, 193-
        195
    games by skill-level 187t
    modifications 186-187t
    reverse turns 181-184, 187-192
    student functional profiles 186
    Web sites 214

Slide Over 171
special education
    communication with teachers of
        197-199
    legal issues 3-6
Special Olympics Web site 214
Spin City I 53
Spin City II 54
Spinning the Ball 46-47
Spinning Wheels I 39-40
Spinning Wheels II 40
Spinning Wheels III 41
Stationary 48-49, 85
Step to Throw I 168-169
Step to Throw II 169
Step to Throw III 170
Stop the Music I 50-51
Stop the Music II 51
Stop the Music III 52
Strike It Rich I 137
Strike It Rich II 139-140
Strike It Rich III 141

T

Table Target Pass I 106
Table Target Pass II 107
Table Target Pass III 107-108
Tabletop Tennis 137-138
Tap and Go 187-188
Target Toss 44-45, 81
Tarzan Attack I 108
Tarzan Attack II 109
Tarzan Attack III 109-110
Tarzan Tennis 138-139
teachers, communicating with 197-
    199
Throw It Out I 163
Throw It Out II 163-164
Throw It Over I 117, 121-122
Throw It Over II 118
Triangle and Go 34, 35, 37

U

Up and Over I 116
Up and Over II 116-117
Up It Goes 162-163

W

The Wall 120
Wall to Net 144
The Weave 193
Web sites, disability sports 214
wheelchair basketball

about 17-20t
ball movement skills 27-30, 42-43,
    54-56
dribbling skills 23-25, 48-50
game descriptions for low-
    functioning students 32t-43
game descriptions for moderate-
    to high-functioning students
    43-56, 44t
games by skill-level 32t, 44t
modifications for 31t-32
passing skills 21-23, 33-34, 44-46
pivoting skills 39-41, 52-54
shooting skills 25-27, 34-37, 46-48
stopping skills 37-39, 50-52
student functional profiles 30-31t
Web sites 214
wheelchair racquetball Web site 214
wheelchairs
    backward propulsion 10, 13
    fitting 210t-212
    forward propulsion 8-9, 12
    frame design 208-209
    obtaining additional 215
    pivoting (spins) 10-12, 13
    stopping 9, 13
    types 206-208
    wheels 206-208
Wheelchair Sports Web site 214
wheelchair tennis
    about 125-129, 128t
    backhand 131-132, 139-141, 144-
        145, 146-147
    equipment 216
    forehand 130-131, 137-139, 144-
        145, 146-147
    game descriptions for low-
        functioning students 136t-143
    game descriptions for moderate-
        to high-functioning students
        143t-147
    games by skill-level 136t, 143t
    grip 129, 130
    modifications 135t
    serving 133-134, 141-143, 144,
        145-146, 147
    student functional profiles 135t
    Web sites 214
Work It Across 175

Z

Zigzag Relay 167
Zigzag Tennis 140-141

About the Author

Ronald W. Davis, PhD, is a professor of adapted physical education at Ball State University. He has two decades of experience teaching, researching, and serving as an advocate for people with disabilities in physical education. A former disability sports coach and referee, he was director of athlete classification in the 1996 Atlanta Paralympics. He was also a project director for three professional preparation training grants from the United States Department of Education.

Dr. Davis has published extensively throughout the world and is considered an expert on teaching people with disabilities. He served as president of AAHPERD's Adapted Physical Activity Council and won AAHPERD's Adapted Physical Education Program of the Year award in 2001.

Photo Courtesy of Brerdan Meehan